The English Langua

For Murray Forbes

The English Language in Scotland

An Introduction to Scots

CHARLES JONES

TUCKWELL PRESS

First published in Great Britain in 2002 by

Tuckwell Press
The Mill House
Phantassie
East Linton
East Lothian EH40 3DG
Scotland

The publishers thank the Scotland Inheritance Fund
for their support in the publication of this volume

ISBN 1 86232 206 6

British Library Cataloguing in Publication Data
A catalogue record for this book is available
on request from the British Library

Typeset in Stone by Koinonia, Manchester
Printed and bound by Bell & Bain Ltd, Glasgow

Contents

Aims and Objectives

This *Introduction* has a quite limited set of objectives and aims. Primarily it sets out to provide a general overview of the linguistic characteristics of Modern Scots and its history. There is a serious shortage of introductory books and monographs on the linguistic and cultural characteristics of the English language as it is and has been spoken and written in Scotland. A short work like this may go some way towards providing some of the academic underpinning in the subject both for the university student and interested layperson.

This book sets out to describe the grammar (in the widest sense) of the English language as it is spoken in Scotland today together with its historical development and evolution. The grammatical study will embrace topics such as syntax (sentence structure), morphology (word structure), sounds and pronunciations and vocabulary. These various elements of the grammar will be placed within a wide context of usage to reflect the ways in which they manifest themselves in the various geographical regions of the country as well as the ways they react to non-linguistic phenomena such as social class and gender.

The historical discussion will examine both the external (social, political and religious) factors which have influenced change in the language through time (and which may well be ongoing today). This discussion will highlight a selection of the historical linguistic mechanisms which have produced the identifying features of the modern language.

This *Introduction* assumes that the user has only a moderate knowledge of the intricacies of linguistic theory and terminology and it has, therefore, attempted to keep such elements at an absolute minimum throughout. However, there are places where terminological knowledge and theoretical insight are unavoidable if anything meaningful has to be made of the data, which are often very complex. While a minimal-terminology stratagem has gains in accessibility and readability, it loses, of course, in detail and accuracy of both observation and description. The bibliographical materials added at the end of each chapter are meant to at least alleviate this kind of problem as well as provide further avenues of investigation for individual topics. A more inclusive bibliography of works relating to the study of the English language in Scotland is appended to the book.

The reader may find some of the descriptions and claims made in the *Introduction*, especially those relating to the very nature of what we are describing – the English language in Scotland or Scots – sometimes controversial. I have tried to take a 'broad church' approach to the language wherever possible although, in essence, what is described in this book is the English used in Scotland now and in the past by real speakers in face-to-face situations. However, there is a strong case to be made too for the use of that same language in literary and other written contexts, and some of the issues relating to these are also raised and discussed.

Any writer of an introductory work of this kind must obviously depend heavily upon the work of many other scholars. I am very conscious of the debt I owe to the many Scots language experts whose researches have enabled this work to be possible, although any misinterpretations or misrepresentations of their views in this book must lie at my door. My thanks are in particular due to Professor A. Fenton and Dr Christine Robinson for the many helpful and insightful comments they made on the draft versions of this book. I should like to express my appreciation here too to Murray Forbes and the Navigator Foundation of Boston for their unstinting financial and moral support for Scots language studies at Edinburgh University. My thanks are due too to Dr Keith Williamson of the Linguistic Atlas of Late Middle English at Edinburgh University for his kind offer to produce the Dialect Map.

CHAPTER ONE

The Study of Scots – Wir Ain Leid?

What is meant by the term 'Scots' when it is used in a linguistic context? The issue generates considerable debate and there seems to be little agreement as to what criteria can be used to define precisely what type of linguistic entity Scots is. Indeed, some of the positions taken on the subject have become quite polarised. Perhaps the most neutral description of the linguistic entity called Modern Scots is as *the principal linguistic medium of face-to-face communication used by the vast majority of speakers who live within the boundaries of Scotland today.* Other definitions are, of course, current, notably those which include the largely artificial and reconstructed version of the English spoken in Scotland in the sixteenth and seventeenth centuries and revived in the early part of the twentieth century. This variety is sometimes known as **Lallans** (Lowland Scots) and it is not only used by many modern writers of prose and, more particularly perhaps, poetry but is also the form espoused and proselytised by organisations such as the Scots Language Society and the Scots Language Resource Centre. Important and influential as these literary and reconstructed varieties of Scots are, their description falls largely outside the scope of this *Introduction*, although reference will be made to them from time to time. Useful publications emanating from organisations such as the Scots Language Society are readily available. This *Introduction* will be mainly concerned with an exploration of the characteristics of the linguistic medium which represents the daily spoken and written form of the English language peculiar to Scotland, both as regards its current features and those that have typified its historical development from the time of its earliest records. Throughout we shall refer to this medium as **Scots**.

To a limited extent, Scotland is a multi-lingual speech community. There are still numerous speakers of Scottish **Gaelic** –

but they are all bilingual in Gaelic and English. There is, too, a considerable number of speakers of languages from the Indian sub-continent, notably Bangladeshi and Bengali, although in these cases as well, the majority of speakers (with the exception of some of the very old) are probably bilingual in English. The question is often asked as to whether Scots is a *language* or just a *dialect* of English. The use of the term 'just' infers that, somehow, dialects are inferior to 'real' languages, a claim which, if taken seriously, would have unfortunate implications for United States English which, although clearly an English dialect, can hardly be considered inferior to British English. Especially so since it has now become the world's *lingua franca* and has some five or six times more native speakers than does its British counterpart.

The question as to what constitutes a full and distinct language can in many cases be decided by reference to what are purely linguistic criteria: the syntax, phonology and vocabulary of Navaho is so distinct from that of, say, Ki Swahili that there is no sense in which they could be called anything other than completely unique languages at every level. On the other hand, it is true that there are groups of languages that exist in close 'family' relationships with each other. The Germanic languages are a good case in point – German, English, Swedish, Danish, Norwegian, Icelandic and Dutch are quite closely related across a wide range of grammatical criteria and share a common historical development. But they have in the course of time become sufficiently formally distinct from one another to be classified as separate languages. However, within such language families themselves there can be varying degrees of grammatical closeness – Spanish is possibly closer to Italian than it is to another Romance language like French, and Danish is possibly closer to Swedish than it is to, say, German.

But linguistic 'closeness' is perhaps most obvious when we consider regional varieties (**dialects**) of the same language in a given speech community. Although there are obvious differences between the pronunciation and (to a less extent) the syntax of the dialects spoken in the English and Scottish

Border counties, they are in general terms still very close to each other at almost every level of their linguistic form. In such a case it would not be appropriate to talk about different languages. Yet we have to bear in mind that the criteria for specifying what constitutes separate and distinct language status are not always based on formal linguistic concerns. The attitudes and political intentions of language users and language planners play a very significant role in this argument. For instance, there are many well-documented instances where – for overtly political reasons – linguistic diversity (of the close, near dialect-level kind) is covered up or suppressed for purely political reasons. This can be seen in the efforts of language planners in the former USSR to refuse to treat the Turkish dialects spoken in Central Asia as Turkish, insisting that they were separate and distinct languages associated with identifiable geographical-political constructs. In western Europe as well there has been a tendency within countries like France (Provençal) and Spain (Catalan) to withhold recognition of what are socially and culturally distinctive language varieties, seeing them as mere variants of 'proper' French or Spanish. So, too, the many divergent types of Arabic tend to be lumped together under a single label, while the very distinctive Mandarin and Cantonese varieties are, again for political and attitudinal reasons, classified together simply as Chinese.

Yet the opposite process can also occur. What are functionally very closely related language types (even dialects) can have their status artificially raised to that of full language, again for social and political reasons. In recent historical times, for example, the Romanian dialect spoken in Moldavia was accorded full language status as Moldovan, while a similar process can be seen today in attempts to give separate language status to Slavic dialects like Croatian and Serbian in the Balkans. All such attempts represent purely politically driven mechanisms which (at least in part) represent the attitudes, allegiances and perceptions of speakers on the ground (but not necessarily those from outside the communities affected).

An issue not unlike this has, in recent times, affected the status of the English spoken in Scotland. There are many people who consider that such a regional variety deserves the status of a full language, rather than being classified as a dialect. The reasons given for this position are rarely structural, in that there is little attempt made to show differences between Scots and English in syntax, morphology and phonology sufficiently substantial to raise the former to a full language status. (The same kind of controversy currently also takes place concerning the status of Low German relative to German proper.) The reasons proposed for considering Scots as a full-blown language are usually political, historical and cultural. The fact that this version of English was once spoken in what was a nation state, has been spoken for a very long period of time there and has a considerable literary culture associated with it is, for some, sufficient reason to classify Scots as a language distinct in its own right from English. Such attitudinal views are extremely powerful and are often overtly expressed by language users. For instance, while there is probably as great a divergence from Standard English in the dialect of English spoken in Dorset as there is in that of the North-East of England, the sense of social and cultural cohesion in the latter area makes its speakers especially aware of their dialect as operating as a kind of regional 'language'.

There is a widely held view that Scots has over time become increasingly less 'pure' and, especially over the past three hundred years, become much anglicised, losing its language-specific status as a result. There is often expressed too a desire for a return to some imagined untainted version of Scots, especially of the type spoken in its literary Golden Age of the sixteenth century. There are, of course, serious problems inherent in such views. In the first place, language change is inevitable and unstoppable, and even if Scots were to have had no contact with English at all in the past centuries, there is little likelihood that it would have remained unchanged. There is no doubt, of course, that there has been an increased and increasing accommodation between Scots and English in recent times, a more or less one-way accommodation in the direction of English. Yet Scots still remains distinctive and identifiable, in much the same way that the Englishes spoken in New

Zealand or Australia do. It is important to stress too that Scots should be seen not as a single entity, but one which ranges from a very 'broad' regional and social type (like, say, the rural speech of Aberdeenshire or the Working Class usage of Glasgow) to a form which has similarities to Standard English. In other words, the linguistic manifestations of Scots should be seen as a type of scale or cline, encompassing a very broad range of usage and formal characteristics.

There have appeared several movements whose aim it is to recover and preserve what is seen as the true Scots language heritage. These have succeeded in having Scots recognised by the European Charter as one of Europe's traditional minority *languages*. Interestingly, too, this status has been accorded to the form of Scots spoken in Ulster – **Ullans** (Ulster Lallans). Yet language revitalisation through language planning and political *diktat* has in the past had only a very patchy success. The process has a certain degree of artificiality to it – for example Cornish has no surviving native speakers, yet language planners seek to re-establish it without any accurate data as to how it was even pronounced. Even in what looks at first sight to be the more promising case of Irish, here too language revitalisation has had a very chequered history. Despite considerable proselytisation at educational and political levels, the success of the introduction of Irish Gaelic as a national language has been very limited – there are still only about ten thousand speakers who can claim native-speaker status (and most of these are bilingual in English as well).

Language planners often seek to establish the credibility of revitalised languages by inventing for them their own special orthographic form, on the basis that a language can only successfully exist if it has a standard written format (this despite the fact that until very recently the majority of the world's languages had no written form at all). In the case of Scots, an attempt has been made by organisations such as the Scots Language Society to produce just such a standard orthography for what they perceive as the uniquely identifiable language – Scots. A sample of the format they propose is:

There is sic a thing as badly spelled Scots, faur oot o onie acceppit staundard. Whiles guid leiterature braks throu menseless spellin, but we hae tae mind at non-conformance tae existin norms is a bar tae readin wi fluency an pleisure, whan the ee's interruptit wi ower monie sair bits. Scots, a thraetened leid, needs tae bide closs tae its sources o authenticity in the speak o the fowk, an thair wey o speakin differs a kennin frae here tae thonder. This disnae mak a guid system impossible, but suggests at the smeddum o the system soud be tae prefer the meinimal, maist-encompassin form tae unnecessar parteicularism an owerspellin. Thus the chiel drauchtin this sentence o the report haes been persuadit bi the Comatee's discussion no tae use the obvious *yaise*, an pit oot o uiss the *yiss* at is sae kenspeckle in Central Scotland scrievin. He ettles tae desist frae endin negative verbs wi –nae, an haes gane ower tae –na acause it sers the mair open soond o the Aest ithoot cowpin the Wastern soondin o't.

The difficulties associated with such attempts at revival and retention through the standardisation of orthographies are many. In the first place, we need to ask just what group of native Scots speakers in Scotland today uses language like this? How many current speakers of Modern Scots would be able to understand what this orthography meant if it were to be shown to them? What is meant by the 'authenticity of the speech of the people'? Which regional or social dialect is such orthography meant to represent? How many speakers of Scots would be happy to hold a conversation in the kind of language represented in this quotation? The existence of an orthography for non-standard dialects can often make matters more complex for their 'survival', since speakers very often do not recognise the proposed spelling system as a type of the dialect they themselves speak on a daily basis

There remains too the problem of specialised, technical and scientific vocabulary. Very often the effects of language change on regional dialects has meant that their original vocabularies have become severely depleted – words for new concepts and technologies have to be taken from a related, but perceived as more culturally dominant, language. Language planners very often solve this problem by putting older vocabulary to a new, modern use, but this often has the effect of de-intellectualising the language, making it in the process unattractive to users of the standard form. One ends up very often with what looks like a 'hamely tongue', one which fails to be taken completely seriously when used in scientific and other specialised contexts.

But none of this means that the distinctive quality of an important regional variant of English like Modern Scots need in any way be compromised. We only need to look at New Zealand, Australia and the United States to see that there are many ways of showing dialectal divergence from a related language (either written or spoken) without recourse to the resurrection of archaic vocabulary, pronunciations or syntactic/morphological devices. It is with such characteristics that we will be concerned in this *Introduction*, with respect to both the history and current usage of the variety of English known as Scots, a variety of English which has been used in face-to-face and written communication in Scotland for the past fourteen hundred years.

Suggested Reading

(Items marked * are those which are most strongly recommended as an introduction to the basic concerns of each section).

*Aitken, A.J. 1981. 'The Good Old Scots Tongue: does Scots have an identity?', in E. Haugen, J.D. McClure and D. Thomson. eds. *Minority Languages Today*. Edinburgh. Edinburgh University Press, pp. 72–90.

Aitken, A.J. 1979. 'Scottish Speech: a historical view, with special reference to the Standard English of Scotland', in *Languages of Scotland*, A.J. Aitken and T. McArthur. eds. Edinburgh. Chambers, pp. 85–99.

Aitken, A.J. 1973. ed. *Lowland Scots*. Aberdeen. Association for Scottish Literary Studies. Occasional Papers 2.

Cheyne, W.M. 1970. 'Stereotype reactions to speakers with Scottish and English Regional Accents', *British Journal of Social and Clinical Psychology* 9, pp. 77–79.

Craigie, W.A. 1950. 'Scottish Language', in *Chambers' Encyclopaedia*, New Edition.

Görlach, M. 1985. ed. *Focus on Scotland*. Amsterdam. Benjamins.

Hardie, K. 1995. 'Scots: matters of identity and nationalism', *Scottish Language* 14/15, pp. 141–147.

*Kay, B. 1993. *Scots: the Mither Tongue*. Alloa. Darvel.

Macafee, C.I. 1985. 'Nationalism and the Scots Renaissance Now', in M. Görlach. ed. *Focus on Scotland. Varieties of English Around the World*. Amsterdam. Benjamins, pp. 7–17.

Mather, J.Y. 1973. 'The Scots we speak today', in A.J. Aitken. ed. *Lowland Scots*. Aberdeen. Association for Scottish Literary Studies. Occasional Papers 2, pp. 56–68.

*Murison, D. 1985. *The Guid Scots Tongue*. Edinburgh. Mercat Press.

Price, G. 1984. *The Languages of Britain*. London. Edward Arnold, pp. 186-193.

*Romaine, S. 1982. 'The English Language in Scotland', in R.W. Bailey and M. Görlach. eds. *English as a World Language*. Ann Arbor. University of Michigan Press, pp. 56–83.

CHAPTER TWO

The Syntax of Modern Scots

The kinds of sentence and clause structures we are familiar with in standard written English are often found in a 'non-standard' form in various regional and social varieties of the language (although they are arguably perhaps less numerous than pronunciation variants). Modern Scots is no exception to this and syntactic structures like those in 'gonnae no dae that?' ('please desist from doing that' (!)) and 'How no?' ('Why not?') can be found in daily use among many of its speakers (and, indeed, in some informal written language as well). Such 'non-standard' usage illustrates the need to stress the *caveat* that it is unhelpful to deal with syntax (as it is equally unhelpful with pronunciation) as if it were an autonomous concept unrelated to wider linguistic influences such as the geographical area to which the speaker belongs, as well as the speaker's social class, age and gender. No less so is it unhelpful to deal with syntax divorced from considerations relating to the formality level of the situation within which the speaker is using it (either written or spoken). Nevertheless, while we shall attempt to keep these and other issues in mind during our discussion, it is possible to highlight some characteristics of Modern Scots syntax which tend to make it distinct from the standard written English we find in books, newspapers and official documents. There is not space here to deal in detail with every idiosyncratic feature of the syntax of Modern Scots, so we shall limit our discussion to a consideration of noun and pronoun structure, verb structure (especially tense and mood) and the ways in which negative sentences are formed.

2.1. *The Noun Phrase*

The term **Phrase** is used to describe what is usually a group of words, one of which is the most important as far as the meaning of the phrase itself is concerned. Thus, in a group of words like 'the nice old man', it is the word (noun) 'man' which is the central meaningful element (the word which is being talked about and the one which the other words in the phrase comment upon or modify). Such a phrase in which the noun is the head is often referred to as the **Noun Phrase**.

2.1.1. The Definite Article

The definite and indefinite articles 'the' and 'a' have several functions in the Noun Phrase in Standard English. In sentences such as 'The boy is good at grammar' and 'A boy is good at grammar' the 'the'/'a' contrast denotes that in the first sentence both speaker and hearer know the boy in question at some level, while in the second some unspecified individual (not necessarily known to the speaker or hearer) is referred to. This shared knowledge aspect perhaps underlies the Scots use of the definite article in such phrases as 'The Bhoys', 'The Gers', 'The Jags', 'The Jambos' where not only is group membership known, but group allegiance shared. However, it is still possible in some varieties of Modern Scots to find the definite article used in a similar non-standard way, in particular where the items referred to are broadly definable as *institutions* or social establishments (perhaps like the football teams above), the knowledge of whose existence is shared between speaker and hearer/reader. Thus we can find sentences like: 'I am going to the shops for the messages'; 'John's gone to the doctor's with the cold'; 'Bill supports the Celtic'; 'John's in the hospital sick'. Standard English would not show the definite article in such contexts, thus 'John's in hospital sick'. In much the same way, it pays dividends not to fall foul of 'the Glasgow Polis' and, while 'going to the Kirk on Sunday' is often recommended, 'losing the heid' is not. Usage like this is perhaps more prevalent among Working Class speakers, who have also been recorded as using expressions such as 'the day's paper'; 'I'm going to the shops for the milk'; 'I'm going to the pub the night'. In these cases there is no suggestion that such sentences are to be interpreted, say, like 'I am going to the shops we went to last week, not the ones we went to last month', but rather as 'I am going shopping' where no specific shop is identified, or where both speaker and hearer know precisely which shops are referred to in the discourse or, more probably, that some abstract concept relating to a place where goods can be bought is being alluded to. This usage is widespread (and possibly spreading) and we can find definite articles used quite frequently in Modern Scots in situations like: 'Bill's now down with the cold/the 'flu/the chickenpox' and even 'the both of them went to the bingo last night'.

2.1.2. Nouns of Measure and Distance

When signalling the concept of 'more-than-one' (the *plural*), Standard English requires nouns to show plural **morphology**. This usually involves the addition of an additional component to the noun – in this case of a suffix or ending in -s, marking the plural. Thus 'five miles long' and 'twenty ounces of silver'. For many speakers of Modern Scots, however, the addition of the plural marker is redundant in nouns denoting *measure* or *distance*. So we find phrases like: 'five mile long'; 'he weighs fifteen stone'; 'I met my wife ten year ago' and 'Glasgow is twenty mile away'. This usage is perhaps becoming less common today than before and may be becoming mostly confined to older speakers. Not unrelated to this is the loss of the 'of' preposition in phrases denoting *quantity*. Thus, for the Standard English 'a piece of bread', some Scots speakers may produce 'a bit bread'. Likewise we can still come across usage like 'a drop whisky' and, although it must surely be recessive, a phrase like 'a wheen other ploy' has been recorded among non-urban speakers in some geographical regions. But constructions like this are strictly limited to particular items, such as 'bread' and 'whisky', and there seems to be no active tendency to generalise the usage to include phrases like 'a lump steel', 'a sheet metal' or 'a strip silver'.

It is worth mentioning here too that occasionally even in Modern Scots we can find the plurals of nouns formed in ways that are now redundant in Standard English and most varieties of urban Scots. While the main means whereby plurality (more-than-oneness) is expressed is through the addition of an 's' suffix, Standard English occasionally utilises the device of adding an 'n' suffix to perform this task (a device much more common in earlier English), thus 'oxen' and 'children'. Some versions of Scots still retain this practice, showing *shoon* for 'shoes' and *een* for 'eyes'. Another device for plural formation (again more common in earlier stages of the language) involves vowel-change between the singular and plural form: thus 'man'/'men' and 'foot'/'feet'. Scots retains this mechanism in a word like 'cow' whose plural, in several varieties of Scots, can be *kye* – or even the double plural (with 'n' suffix *and* vowel change) as in *kyne*.

2.1.3. Demonstratives

Demonstratives are words placed next to nouns to indicate their place in space or time in relation to the speaker/hearer. In a sentence like 'This book is mine, that one is yours' one of the functions of the 'this'/'that' contrast is to show that the first book is close in space to the speaker, the other, further away. Such a contrast exists in Modern Scots as well (although the form of 'that' is occasionally reduced to *at*). Some social and regional varieties of Modern Scots also show non-standard forms of the plural versions of 'this' and 'that' in *thir* 'these' and *thae* 'those'. The former is possibly becoming residual, although the latter is still quite common, as in: 'See thae muggers, they should be put in the jail'; 'Thae yins is always causin bother'. Although it is probably now rare as well, some speakers can use *them* for 'thae'/'those' in such a context: 'Them boys is always takin liberties'. In common with some other British English dialects, Modern Scots also has an additional demonstrative word in *yon* or *thon* (sometimes *yonder*, *thonner* or *thonder*). The function of this demonstrative seems to be to show that the noun in question is even further away from the speaker than when it is used with the 'that' demonstrative. Thus 'this/that/yon pen is Bill's' can signify an increasing distance of the pen from the speaker.

2.1.4. Pronouns

These 'substitutes for nouns' show some idiosyncratic characteristics in Modern Scots, in particular at the 'broader' end of
the language's spectrum.

(a) In Standard English there is a singular/plural contrast in
the first person pronoun *(the person speaking)* 'I'/'we' and
'me'/'us'; likewise in the third person *(person spoken about)*
'he/she/it' versus 'they'. On the other hand, there is no
contrast between singular and plural second personal
pronouns *(person spoken to)*, both of which are, in Standard
English, simply 'you'. However, in many versions of
Modern Scots (as well as in North-Eastern dialects of
England) a *yous* form can be used in the plural, both in the
subject case ('the doer of the action') – 'Yous is no getting
another drink' – and object ('the done to or the affected')
case – 'I saw yous (lads) at the game last night'. This *yous*
form is also to be found in Ulster Scots, from where it may
have originated, and it now seems to be spreading rapidly
from Glasgow across the Central Belt. Perhaps less commonly than in the past, some speakers will use *you all* for
the plural of the second person, as in: 'Were you all at the
pictures last night?'

(b) The possessive pronoun 'my' has also a non-standard
variant in Modern Scots – *mines*: 'That book is mines' where
the possessive ending in words like 'yours' and 'John's' has
become generalised.

(c) Although it is almost certainly now dying out, there is
evidence that there were pronunciations like [tu], [du] and
[ðu] for 'you' in some regions. The [ðu] 'thoo' types were
associated with the Black Isle district, while the [tu] 'too'
type was identified with the town of Paisley in Renfrew-
shire, where there was even a comic paper entitled the
Seestu: 'see you'.

(d) Standard English reflexive pronouns like 'myself', 'himself',
'themselves' are anomalous; in the 'myself' instance, the
'my' form is a possessive ('belonging to me') while in the
other instances the pronoun is in a locative (directional)

13

form: 'to him'; 'from her'; 'with them'. Many Scots speakers (as also many regional English speakers) generalise the possessive form throughout, producing, on the analogy of 'myself', forms like *hisself* and *theirself/theirselves*.

(e) In some varieties of Scots possessive pronouns can often be used with nouns which in Standard English require no definite article, thus: 'Mary and Henry are going on *their* holidays to Dunoon next year', 'Bill reads the Mail during *his* breakfast'.

2.1.5. *Relative Pronouns and Relative Clauses*

In English, not only can individual words (such as adjectives) modify or comment upon nouns – as in 'the old black cat' – but whole clauses may also act in this way. For example, rather than two sentences like 'The dog was angry' and 'The dog chased the cat', we can combine them into a single sentence, containing two clauses, such that 'The dog, which was angry, chased the cat'. Modifying clauses like 'which was angry' are often referred to as *relative clauses*. There are several forms of words that introduce relative clauses in Standard English – these are known as *relative pronouns*. These reflect the relationship of the pronoun to the verb in its clause (as its subject or its object) as well as the gender/animacy of the noun it stands for or substitutes for. Thus we find: 'The girl who is my sister went home' – *subject*; 'The chair which/that I like appeals to me' – *object*, and 'The woman whose dog bit me has been fined' – *possessor*. Although it is probably now confined to written language only, we can also see a 'whom' form which signals a pronoun in the object case ('that which is affected by the verbal action'), thus: 'The shepherd whom I like saved his sheep'. But this appears to be recessive, even in Standard English. However, Standard English (especially in written usage) shows a 'who'/'that' contrast, depending upon the nature of the relative clause itself. There are two kinds of relative clause, technically known as *non-restrictive* and *restrictive*. In the former the relationship between the relative clause and the main clause can be expressed via an 'and' conjunction: 'My brother, who is forty-five, likes Twix' means that my brother (and) who happens to be forty-five also likes Twix. On the other hand a sentence like 'The girl who/that liked Twix was sent home' means that from among the several girls who are present, it is the one who likes Twix who is sent home – an individual from a set of individuals – the *restrictive* relative clause type. Note too how this latter type has a different intonational pattern from the non-restrictive.

At the broad end of the language spectrum, Scots speakers can use relative words like *at* 'that'; *whae* 'who'; *wham* 'whom'; *whase* 'whose'; and *whilk* 'which'. But perhaps the outstanding characteristic of formal written and spoken Scots is the way in which it limits the relative word to the 'that' form in both restrictive and non-restrictive contexts, thus: 'It was the bloke that was drunk that was banned from driving'; 'They are the folk that we had dinner with last night'. It should be noted too that in some varieties of Scots (as in several other regional British dialects) the speaker will use a conjunction 'and' to join two connected clauses where otherwise a relative clause construction would be used. Thus, a sentence like 'The man who we saw yesterday sold me the car' can be realised as 'We saw the man yesterday and he sold me the car'. Fairly typical of Scots too is the use of 'trace' or 'shadow' pronouns, as in 'The town I hadn't been *there* for several months' rather than the standard 'The town in which I hadn't been for several months'. So, too, cases like: 'The girls you see at the disco and try to chat *them* up'.

There are also regional versions of Scots where it is still possible to find *that's* forms for 'whose', as in 'The cat that's kittens were born last week', and 'The students that's books were stolen last week are very upset', for 'whose books were stolen'.

2.2. *The Verb Phrase*

The Verb Phrase is a group of words containing, as its head word, a verb – the indicator of the type and character of the activity involved in the sentence. Thus, a Verb Phrase might look like 'may have eaten', where the head word 'eat' is modi-fied, or commented upon by other 'auxiliary' words like 'may' and 'have' + 'en', the former denoting possibility/permission (a *modal* verb), the latter that the activity of eating is com-pleted and not ongoing (the *past participle*). The verb itself may be modified in various ways in order to express the *time* of the action (its *tense*) or its *state of completion or incompletion* (its *aspect*). Thus 'John kisses Mary' (present) and 'Zebedee kissed Dougal at three o'clock' (past) versus 'Zebedee had kissed Dougal by two o'clock' (action completed, expressed through the use of the *past participle*, denoted by the use of an auxiliary verb 'has'/'have' and a suffix in '–en' on the verb itself). Verbal aspect in English and Scots can also indicate that an activity is ongoing or incomplete, 'Zebedee is still kissing Florence' by means of the *present participle*, a combination of verb and '–ing' suffix.

2.2.1. Tense and Time marking

Standard English morphology and syntax tend to mark only two time references: the *now* and the *before-now* (traditionally the present and the past tense), as in 'she goes now' as against 'she went yesterday'. The language has two main stratagems for showing that the verbal activity is in the past: (a) by alter-ing the stressed vowel of the verb itself – thus 'they sit' versus 'they sat' or, and more commonly, by appending a suffix (usually spelt <ed> or <t> and pronounced [t], [d] or [əd]), as in 'he looked', 'she dragged' and 'they parted'. Of course, there are several other scenarios as well, one, for instance, where the past-tense form shows a *combination* of both stratagems: 'I think' versus 'I thought', 'I keep'/'I kept' and yet other occa-sions when a different verb form altogether is used: 'I go' versus 'I went' and 'I make'/'I made'.

For the English language in general, it is the dental suffix-adding type that is what is known as the 'productive' model for past tense signalling. Even young children learning the lan-guage will generalise this type and produce 'I seed' and 'I goed'. Many of the broader varieties of Modern Scots do this too, and we find 'he seed'/ 'he saw', 'she drawed'/'she drew', 'I selt it'/'I sold it', 'he catched it'/ 'he caught it' and 'I kneeled' for 'I knelt'. However, occasionally too Scots speakers will generalise the vowel change type, and realise 'I brought' as 'I brung'. Quite commonly, Scots usage will use the past-participle form of the verb for the past tense, so that, instead of a paradigm like 'I see', 'I saw' and 'I have seen', we get 'I see' and a past tense 'I seen'; rather than 'I sink', 'I sank' and 'I have sunk' we find a present tense 'I sink' and a past tense 'I sunk'; as well as 'I give'/ 'I gave'/'I have given' we find 'I give'/'I gave'/'I have gave'. But perhaps the most commonly commented upon example of this practice is the present/past contrast of 'I do'/'I done' rather than the standard three-way contrast of 'I do'/'I did' and 'I have done', as in the much-cited phrase 'the boy done well'.

Yet on occasion, the opposite can occur, and it is the form of the past tense which replaces that of the past participle, so that we get 'I go', 'I went', 'I have went' (instead of 'I have gone'); 'I see', 'I saw', 'I have saw'; and 'I take', 'I took' and 'I have took'.

In Scots and in (especially Northern) English, the historically earlier form of the present participle (as in: *going, seeing, doing*) was with the suffix '-ande', rather than the now standard '-ing'. The earlier form is still to be found in Modern Scots, although it is confined to dialects like Caithness and the far South-West of the country (probably used mainly by older speakers in these areas), so that we can find 'I was findan' for 'I was finding' and 'I was thinkan' for 'I was thinking'.

2.2.2. Modal Verbs

Verbs like 'will', 'shall', 'must', 'may', 'could' and 'would' not only perform a wide range of functions in English, but behave in an irregular and often anomalous fashion both in the standard language as well as in Modern Scots. Their usage is very complex and we shall only be able to list a few idiosyncratically Scots forms here.

Modal verbs like **'shall'** and **'will'** express several different semantic concepts. For example, a sentence like 'I will see my mother tomorrow' involves the speaker in making a *prediction* about an event which may or may not occur (most traditional grammars erroneously call this usage the 'future tense'). The modal 'shall' can also be used in this context with the same meaning, although, if the speaker wishes to stress the *certainty* of the prediction ('it is definitely the case that') then 'shall' is often preferred in Standard English over 'will'. A very salient characteristic of Scots, and one which has been in the language for several hundred years, is its preference for the 'will' modal in both these contexts, 'shall' hardly ever being selected.

The modal verb **'may'** infers, among several other meanings, that the speaker is giving some overt *permission* for some event to occur. Thus 'They may go to the cinema on Friday' can mean, in Standard English, that 'I (the speaker) give permission for some third party to go to the cinema'. Scots generally avoids this usage, preferring to use 'can' or 'get to'. In other words, for a sentence like 'You may go to the swimming pool tomorrow' we can find Scots speakers saying 'you get to go to the swimming pool' or, more usually, 'you can go to the swimming pool'. Again, where 'may' in Standard English infers possibility (rather than permission), as in 'you may or you may not go golfing tomorrow, depending on the weather', Scots avoids 'may' in this context, preferring 'could' or 'might', as in 'Celtic might not win the league again next year'.

In addition to connoting possibility and permission, modal verbs also express *obligation* and *necessity* meanings, particularly through the use of **'ought to'** or **'must'**. Thus 'you really ought to visit your parents at least once a month'. In cases like this, Scots speakers prefer 'should' or even 'want to': 'you want to stop smoking as soon as possible, in my opinion'. A modal like 'must' in Standard English signals some kind of 'logical necessity', as in 'this story must be true, if these facts are correct'. However, in Scots, this usage is generally avoided, a preference being given to the expression 'have to be': 'this story has to be true, if these facts are correct'. Among older speakers in some regions of the country, and certainly in literary materials, the Scots form 'maun' for 'must' can be used: 'Nae man can tether Time nor Tide,/The hour approaches Tam maun ride' (Burns: *Tam O'Shanter*). In Standard English, it is not generally possible to find a negative form of the 'must' modal: **'mustn't'**. However, there is no such constraint in Scots and we regularly hear speakers use sentences like: 'The facts are clearly wrong, so the report's conclusions mustn't be true', where Standard English would prefer 'cannot'.

But perhaps the most characteristic idiosyncrasy of Scots modal usage lies in the fact that two of these verbs *can occur in the same sentence*. For example, it is impossible to have a construction in Standard English in which two modal verbs appear in the same verb phrase as in: 'She might could have done it'. However, such expressions are possible in Scots, so that we can find: 'The teacher will can tell you when the class is over'; 'My father, he'll can go to the match tomorrow' and 'If we behave ourselves, we might can get home early'. These **double modal** constructions occur too in negative sentences such as 'She'll no can give us coffee the day' and 'They might no could swim a length'. This double modal usage is, however, not entirely confined to Scots, but also occurs in North-Eastern dialects of England (especially in the Newcastle area) and in certain parts of the Southern United States.

The double modal usage is extremely complex, as we have already suggested, allowing differential constructions like 'She might no could have done it'/'She might could no have done it' as well as double negations such as 'He shouldnae could no have come'. However, nearly all these double modal constructions are relatively rare, dialectally specific and possibly coming to be recessive in the modern language.

Entirely confined to Scots is the use of the **to-infinitive** with modal verbs ('to can'/'to could'), a construction which is grossly ungrammatical in almost every other English language variety. Scots speakers are likely to say 'I'd like to could do that', 'You have to can write well to be a journalist' and 'I didnae used to could like St Mirren at all'.

2.2.3. Negation

In general, Scots (like Standard English) creates **negative sentences** by inserting a negative word ('not') immediately following an auxiliary (usually the verb 'do') or modal verb; thus 'John saw Mary' becomes 'John didn't see Mary'; 'John will/may see Mary' becomes 'John will not/may not see Mary'. Obviously, too, the negative word can become attached (technically **'cliticised'**) to the modal or auxiliary itself; thus 'John didn't see Mary' and 'John won't see Mary' and so on. Alternatively, a modal like 'will' itself can be cliticised to the sentence's subject, so that 'I will not go to the match' becomes 'I'll not go to the match'. All of these possibilities exist for Scots as well, only the pronunciation form of the negative word being changed from 'not' to 'nae' or 'no'. Thus we can find negative constructions like 'John didnae do that'; 'John willnae do that' and 'John'll no do that'. The 'nae/no' types are Working Class forms in the main and are avoided by Middle Class speakers on nearly all occasions (see §5.2; pp. 51–53).

In Standard English, the negative word 'never' is used to denote 'not at any time' or 'at no time', as in 'my cat never returned from her wanderings'. However, in Scots, 'never' can be used as an equivalent to the 'normal' negative construction, so that for 'John didn't get married' we can find 'John never got married'.

However, it is interesting to note that for many speakers of Modern Scots (again mainly Working Class speakers) it is possible to use the negative word immediately following a main verb like 'have' without the need to involve the 'do' auxiliary. Thus, as well as the negative of a sentence like 'John had a car' being 'John didn't have a car', some speakers of non-standard Scots can say 'John hadnae a car', and one has heard sentences like 'I hated that toon 'cos it hadnae a pub in it'. Likewise mainly confined to Working Class (predominantly male) speakers is the use of **multiple negations**, so that one can come across sentences like 'I just couldnae get parked naewhere' and 'she couldnae dae nothin aboot it'. Sometimes (although the usage is probably confined to older, non-urban speakers) we can also see a negative version – *nor* – of the comparative word 'than': 'He didnae get nae mair nor three quid for his auld car'.

Typical of Working Class usage too is the special use of the verb 'to be' when cliticised with a negative word. Speakers can be heard using 'I amnae good at sums' and 'I'm going to the disco with Mary, amn't I?' Again, in constructions like this last example, where the speaker uses a 'tag' to confirm what has been stated in the main sentence, Scots uses *intit?*, as in 'it's cauld the day, intit?' A favoured tag, especially among Working Class Glaswegians, is the sound [e], and we find speakers saying for 'It's cauld intit?', 'It's cauld, e?'. So too when the context is negative, we find, 'Your goin' tae see the Gers on Saturday, e no?'.

In place of the Standard English 'not at all' construction – as in an (unlikely) phrase such as 'Partick Thistle cannot play football at all' – we find the use of *nane*: 'They Jags can play nane'.

2.2.4. Prepositions

These small words are used in Noun Phrases often to denote direction, place or time: 'in'; 'into'; 'at'; 'before'; 'with' etc. and their usage varies quite considerably between many varieties of Scots and Standard English. Most particularly, Scots uses a different form of preposition from its English counterpart, thus: 'Tom got married on Mary', 'Hamish threw the book ower the window' for 'out of'; 'Mhairi cried on Bill to sit down' for 'called to'. Prepositions like *afore* 'before', *aneath* 'beneath', *aside* 'beside', *ahin* 'behind', *ayoynt* 'beyond' and *atween* 'between' illustrate the use of the Scots prefix a-/an- for the Standard English 'be-'. The now rare (at least in conversational contexts) Scots preposition *anent* or *fornent* means 'opposite' or 'over against': 'whan she kent I had to sit for sae lang fornent sae mony folk'. So too some speakers can still use *aboon* for 'above': 'they waded in the river aboon the knee'.

Suggested Reading

Brown, K. 1991. 'Double Modals in Hawick Scots', in P. Trudgill and J.K. Chambers. eds. *Dialects of English*. London. Longman, pp. 74–103.

*Brown, K. and Miller, J. 1982. 'Aspects of Scottish English syntax'. *English World Wide* 3, pp. 3–17.

Brown, K. and Miller, J. 1980. 'Auxiliary Verbs in Edinburgh Speech'. *Transactions of the Philological Society* 78, pp. 81–133.

Grant, W. and Main-Dixon, J. 1921. *Manual of Modern Scots*. Cambridge. Cambridge University Press.

*Macafee, C.I. 1992. 'Characteristics of non-standard grammar in Scotland'. *http://www.abdn.ac.uk/-en1038/grammar.htm*.

*Miller, J. 1993. 'The Grammar of Scottish English', in J. and L. Milroy. eds. *Real English: the Grammar of English Dialects in the British Isles*. London. Longman, pp. 99–138.

Romaine, S. 1980. 'The relative clause marker in Scots English'. *Language in Society* 9, pp. 221–47.

Trudgill, P. and Hannah, J. 1989. eds. *International English: a Guide to Varieties of Standard English*. London. Edward Arnold. Chapter Five.

CHAPTER THREE

The Sounds of Scottish English and their Structure

Foreword

Before using this section, the reader is advised to familiarise him/herself with the phonetic symbols and their sound equivalents which are set out in the *Appendix*.

3.1. Standards and Dialects

Thus far we have been making a simple, two-way contrast between (Modern) Scots and Standard English. We need to think about these labels a little more before examining the peculiarities of the pronunciation of the English language in Scotland. In many parts of the world where English is spoken, there is a recognition that particular varieties have a standard versus a non-standard form, a contrast which very often (but not always) equates with urban versus non-urban, or Middle Class versus Working Class usage. Indeed, very often there is an explicit view that what is involved is really a contrast between standard and dialectal forms of the language: the standard being the prestigious usage, the dialectal, somehow deviant and 'less sophisticated'. Perhaps the two most obvious examples of standard types are Standard English in the United Kingdom and General American in the United States. British Standard English (sometimes called Received Pronunciation) is that variety of (usually pronunciation) associated in the main with the higher echelons of British society. It is the variety used by those considered to be the social elite – those, for example, educated at the great public schools as well as the members of the aristocracy. However, it is also increasingly regarded as the variety favoured by the upper middle classes. It has great prestige even now and, although – like any other variety – it is subject to linguistic change, it is still relatively homogeneous in form regardless of the geographical origin of its users. However, the number of speakers using this variety in the United Kingdom today is extremely small, something less than one percent of the total population.

The question is often posed as to whether the English language in Scotland has such a standard form, a prestige form peculiar to those groups in the country which have a high social profile. Even at the level of casual observation it is clear that, while there indeed seems to be a 'posh', prestigious form of Modern Scots, it is in several important ways different from its Standard English, Received Pronunciation counterpart. While Middle Class speakers in Scotland do use a form of English not at all unlike Standard English when they speak in formal contexts, the same speakers can – and regularly do – revert to more 'broad' forms of Scots (a process known as 'code shifting') when they are in more informal situations. This formal, upper-class version of Scots is often referred to as **Scottish Standard English**. Yet it is probably not as invariable in linguistic form throughout Scotland to the extent that Standard English is (almost) homogeneous in England. Indeed, it might be better to treat the Scottish situation rather differently, as showing several *regional (mainly urban) standard types* – good examples of which might be the prestige dialects of Edinburgh Morningside and Glasgow Kelvinside. But it is important to stress that Scottish Standard English is not simply an imitation of its English counterpart, but has itself evolved as a specifically Scottish standard prestige form from at least the eighteenth century.

The term 'standard' is, of course, unfortunate, since it implies some kind of linguistic, even cultural, superiority over non-standard 'dialectal' types. Such a view is still widely held and heard and often results in the suppression in many classroom contexts of non-standard language in pupils, bringing with it a sense of embarrassment and, ultimately, inferiority. There are no linguistic grounds for any claim that one variety of a language is inherently or linguistically *better* than any other, although, as we shall see in Chapter Six, varieties can be subject to measures of social and contextual *appropriateness*.

3.2. Some Characteristics of Modern Scots Pronunciation

We shall examine a wide range of pronunciation contrasts in our discussions of the social and regional variation in Modern Scots. At this point, however, it might be useful to concentrate upon a small number of salient pronunciations, pronunciations which are often seen as the defining characteristics of the Modern Scots 'accent'. There are around eight or so of these which set Modern Scots Standard pronunciation apart from the pronunciation of Standard English itself.

(1) Perhaps the most salient of all the vowel pronunciations which identify Scots speakers (and one often parodied by those 'putting on' a Scottish accent) is that which occurs in words like 'say' and 'go'. For the Middle Class urban Scots speaker in particular, the vowels in these and similar words are resolutely monophthongal – [se] and [go] – in sharp contrast to the case in Standard English where diphthongal forms [seɪ] and [goʊ] are most frequently to be heard.

(2) Standard English is characterised as showing what is often described as the BATH/TRAP split. In words like 'path', 'after', 'father' and 'pass' a long low *back* [ɑɑ] vowel sound is used in that variety. The phonetic contexts where this occurs are often predictable – i.e. when the sound follow-ing the vowel is a fricative of some kind. On the other hand, in words (especially those ending in a stop sound) like 'hat', 'that', 'tap' and 'mad', the vowel used is the low *front* [a]. (However, even in Standard English itself, there is some variability, some speakers pronouncing words like 'banana' and 'plastic' with either the low front or the low back vowel.) In many varieties of Standard Scottish English this BATH/TRAP split does not operate, speakers generally using the [a] vowel in both instances. However, on occa-sion, many Scots Middle Class speakers accommodate to the Standard English contrast in formal speech contexts.

(3) In Standard English, the vowel sound in words such as 'hit', 'it' and 'thin' is normally a high front [ɪ] sound. How-ever, it is a characteristic of speakers of several varieties of

25

Modern Scots that this vowel is lowered and centralised to a sound not unlike that in a word like 'hull', making 'hill' and 'hull' sound almost alike. This lowered and centralised vowel (whose symbol is [ë]) can be produced by pronouncing the vowel in a word such as 'get' using an exaggerated rounding of the lips. Although this [ë] vowel is more common among low prestige speakers, it is also apparently spreading rapidly into Middle Class usage.

(4) Standard English shows a vowel pronunciation difference between words like 'pool' and 'pull', 'full' and 'fool' and 'pudding'/'brooding'. The spelling of these words suggests that at one time in their history they were quite distinct, and even today speakers of Standard English will show a vowel of a different quality and quantity between the pairs. For instance, a word like 'full' has for such speakers a vowel which sounds like [o] but with the lips spread rather than rounded: the symbol for the sound being [ɤ]. On the other hand, in a word like 'fool' the vowel is the high back rounded [u] and is usually pronounced *long*: [uu]. In other words, there is a qualitative as well as a quantitative (length) distinction between the 'full/fool' pairs. Such a contrast tends not to exist for speakers of Scottish Standard English, who use the same short vowel for both words. While that vowel is usually [u], for many Scots speakers it is fronted to [ü] and shows substantial lip rounding as well. Such a rounded pronunciation is, of course, a hallmark of the Scots Working Class speaker but, as with many such others, it is infiltrating Middle Class usage.

(5) Modern Scots is known as a rhotic language: that is, words spelt with an 'r' at the end of a syllable or word, have that [r]-sound pronounced. Like American English speakers (as well as some English dialect speakers from Lancashire and Devon/Cornwall), Scots speakers will pronounce the [r] in words like 'car', 'far' and 'father'. As we shall see in our section dealing with social matters [§5:pp. 53–54], there are at least three different types of [r] sound used by speakers of Modern Scots, types which serve to identify the social class, age and sex of the speaker. Standard English,

of course, has seen this syllable final [r] sound lost (mainly late in the nineteenth century) and replaced by a vowel sound. Thus, for these speakers, a word like 'fear' ends in a falling diphthong: [fiə], where the [ə] symbol ('schwa') represents the kind of sound heard at the beginning of words like 'about', 'alone'.

One of the important consequences of the fact that Modern Scots retains the syllable final [r] sound is that in words like 'word', 'bird' and 'heard' a *separate* vowel sound is to be heard, thus: [wʌrd], [bɪrd] and [hɛrd]. In Standard English, on the other hand, there is a single shared (long) vowel – [əə] – in all three words.

(6) Words like 'dawn' and 'don'; 'caught' and 'cot' show by their spellings that, at one time in their history, they had separate, distinct pronunciations. This distinctiveness is still clear today in some British English dialects, notably Standard English, where we find pronunciations like [dɒn] 'dawn' and [dɔn] 'Don'. The [ɒ] sound is quite close to the Standard English vowel in 'path' and 'fast' (and is often heard in United States English in words like 'got' and 'Bobby'). The [ɔ] sound is that commonly heard in Scots in words like 'got' and 'not'. This 'dawn'/'don' distinction does not exist in many varieties of Modern Scots at all; instead, there has been a **merger** of the two sounds under that for 'Don', the [ɔ] sound.

(7) 'wh' words. In Scottish Standard English there is a clear and distinct difference in pronunciation between the first sound in words like 'whale', 'which', 'what', 'where' and that in words like 'wail', 'witch', 'watt' and 'wear'. In the former set, Modern Scots speakers (in nearly all dialects) will produce a [hw] sound – [w] preceded by some aspiration or breathing, while in the latter, there is a [w] sound alone. This [hw] (or [ʍ]) versus [w] contrast is not present in Standard English at all, and words like 'whale' and 'wail', 'Wales' and 'whales', 'why' and 'Wye' are homophonous, all showing an initial [w].

(8) One of the most obvious features of the pronunciation of 'non-standard', dialectal Scots is the use of the velar and

palatal fricatives – [x] and [ç] – heard in the way some speakers pronounce 'brought' [brɔxt] and 'night' [nɪçt]. These sounds correspond rather closely to those found in Modern German in words like 'ach' and 'ich'. However, in Scottish Standard English, the palatal fricative is certainly rarely, if ever, used, except perhaps in 'dreich', and the velar fricative is confined to what is really a special and limited set of words, such as 'loch', 'Auchtermuchty' and 'Sauchiehall', and in some personal names like 'Tulloch' and 'Murdoch'. We shall see in a later discussion how both sounds are becoming lost, not only in Scottish Standard English, but in less prestigious varieties as well.

(9) The way in which *vowel length* is assigned is perhaps one of the most distinctive features of Modern Scots as a whole (although similar systems are to be found in other British regional varieties, notably those in the North-East of England and Ulster). Compare the relative duration or length of the high front vowel [i] in the words in the following two lists:

Type A	Type B
Breathe	Keith
Sneeze	Lease
Leave	Leaf
Bee	Leap

For Modern Scots speakers, there is a clear contrast in vowel length between Types A and B. The former have a duration which is audibly longer than the latter, thus [briːð] versus [kiθ], [liːv] versus [lif] and [biː] versus [lip]. (The convention of a double vowel symbol is used here to indicate that the vowel is long. Some works on phonetics use a [ː] mark after the vowel for this purpose, thus [iː].) This distinction in length does not hold nearly to the same extent for speakers of Standard English who – in general – treat all the words as showing a lengthened vowel sound. We might want to ask the question as to what constitutes the mechanism lying behind the Scots speaker's knowledge as to when to make the vowel long or short. Is it just a feat of memory, or are there any recognisable principles which underlie it?

The answer lies in examining the nature of *the kind of sound which follows the vowel*. In those cases where that sound is (1) a *voiced fricative* (such as [ð] or [z]), (2) *[r]* or (3) when *the vowel is itself the last segment in the word*, then the vowel is going to be *long*. In all other contexts (voiceless fricatives, voiced/voiceless stops) it will be short. In other words, the phonetic nature of the final sound in the word determines the length of the vowel which precedes it. The process in question is often referred to as the *The Scottish Vowel Length Rule* and may be summarised as follows:

> *Vowels preceding voiced fricatives, preceding [r] and when word final are long; otherwise they are short.*

The vowels which tend to be affected by this process are principally the high vowels [i] and [u] and there is little, if any, similar or thorough-going similar effect on other vowels like [e], [o] and [a]. It is important to stress that speakers of Modern Scots do not have to 'memorise' the length of vowel sounds: it is entirely predictable by the kind of phonetically conditioned rule described above.

However, we do need to extend the rule to include other kinds of (non-phonetic) influencing factors. Compare the length of the stressed vowels in pairs of words like:

Type A	Type B
brood	brew+ed
greed	agree+d
need	knee+d
nod	gnaw+ed
Healey	free+ly
feline	feel+ing

The words under Type B share a common characteristic: they all involve *morphology*. That is, they all show inflectional endings or suffixes which impart additional meaning to the word in question. Thus 'I brew' present time action, versus 'I brewed' past time action, and so on. Those words under Type B showing morphological endings have their vowels *long*, those under Type A (morphology free) have *short* vowels. Thus, we have to add to *The Scottish Vowel Length Rule* another condition to the effect that *the addition of morphology tends to make the vowel in the word longer.*

The Scottish Vowel Length Rule has yet another characteristic in Modern Scots. This concerns the way it affects the [aɪ] diphthong in words like 'my' and 'tie'. We can perhaps illustrate this by looking at the infamous (and probably apocryphal) football score result: 'East Fife five, Forfar four'. For a speaker of Standard English, the diphthong in both 'Fife' and 'five' would be the same: [aɪ] as in 'my'. However, we observe that these two words are distinguished by one having a voiceless fricative final consonant, the other a final consonant which is voiced. And we noted above how voiced fricatives tend to make the vowel preceding them longer, hence 'maze' with a long vowel and 'mace' with one which is shorter. In the case of 'Fife' versus 'five' it would appear that what is involved is mainly a vowel *quality* (rather than *quantity*) contrast. 'Five' shows an [ae] diphthong in Scottish Standard English (rather than the [aɪ] of Standard English), while 'Fife' has a quite distinctively different [ʌɪ] or [əɪ] type. The difference can be heard too in word parts like 'rise'/'rice'; 'alive'/'life' as well as in other phonetic contexts where *The Scottish Vowel Length Rule* operates: 'writhe'/'write'; 'shy'/'file'. Some scholars have suggested that the Scots [ae]/[ʌɪ] contrast is one of length as well as quality, in the [ae] instance the [a] segment being slightly longer.

Suggested Reading

Abercrombie, D. 1979. 'The Accents of Standard English in Scotland', in *Languages of Scotland*, A.J. Aitken and T. McArthur. eds. Edinburgh, Chambers.

Aitken, A.J. 1981. 'The Scottish Vowel Length Rule', in M. Benskin and M.L. Samuels. eds. *So Meny People Longages and Tongues.* Edinburgh. Edinburgh University Press, pp. 131–157.

Grant, W. 1912. *The Pronunciation of English in Scotland.* Maryland. McGrath.

Leith, D. 1983. 'The Development of Scots', in *A Social History of English.* London. Routledge, pp. 158–164.

Scobbie, J.M., Hewitt, N. and Turk, A.E. 1999. 'Standard English in

Edinburgh and Glasgow: the Scottish Vowel Length rule revealed',
in P. Foulkes and G.J. Docherty. eds. *Urban Voices*. London. Arnold,
pp. 230–245.

Wells, J.C. 1982. *Accents of English 2: The British Isles*. Cambridge.
Cambridge University Press. 5.2 *Scotland*, pp. 393–417.

CHAPTER FOUR

The Vocabulary of Modern Scots:
The Meaning and Structure of Words

4.1. The Scots word-hoard

We should perhaps begin by asking the question as to whether there really is such a thing as a word-cache, a vocabulary, which is specific to Modern Scots and which differs uniquely from the list of words which goes to make up the vocabulary of Standard English. It would seem fairly obvious if we listen to speakers of Modern Scots, when they use the language in conversational contexts, that the bulk of the words they use is, by and large, shared with that of Standard English – although they may have quite different pronunciations. Scots and English share words like *man, dog, bus, sky, mountain*, etc. etc., words which are not included in those dictionaries which deal primarily with Scots vocabulary. On the other hand, it is undoubtedly true that there appear to be large numbers of words whose meaning and usage are strictly confined to Scots contexts, the kinds of words which we find listed in works like *The Concise Scots Dictionary* or *The Scottish National Dictionary*. Indeed, even *The Oxford English Dictionary* will include words which are identified as being Scots or dialectal. A question we must ask too is not just whether these are vocabulary items which are uniquely Scottish, but whether speakers are able to appreciate that they are so and, indeed, whether speakers – once told that such words are Scots – are able to recognise what they mean. These concerns are not, of course, confined to Scots. They hold good for almost any regional dialect of English (or any other language, for that matter). Standard English speakers often cannot identify or will wrongly assign meanings to Yorkshire- or Dorset-specific vocabulary, while – even in the United States – speakers will often misinterpret the meanings of words which are peculiar to specific geographical regions on that continent. The misinterpretations between

British and United States English in items like *boot, fender, sidewalk, pavement, rubber* and *trunk* are well known.

Some of these issues can be illustrated by choosing, at random, pages from *The Concise Scots Dictionary*. Pages 304–305 of this excellent work contain samples of items beginning with the letter <h> and include words which all speakers of English will recognise or, at the very least, be able to guess the meanings of. Such items include *hund, hound, houn* 'a hunting dog'; *hunger* 'hunger, lack of food'; *hurl* 'to hurtle, to fall from a height' and perhaps even *hunker* 'to squat, to sit in a crouching position'. Even *humfie* and *humfy-back* 'hunchbacked' may well be recognised by some speakers as will *hunch* 'an upward thrust of the shoulders'. Indeed, there will be certain segments of the Glasgow community who will recognise (but not, in some cases, necessarily approve of) the definition of *Huns* as 'abusive nickname for Rangers football team'. But what of items such as *humple* 'a small heap or mound'; *hunker-slider* 'a slippery customer'; *hupe* 'circular wooden frame enclosing millstones'; *hurdie* 'hips, buttocks'; *hurk* 'to sit in a crouched position'; *hurkle* 'a horse hoe for cleaning turnips'; *hurcheon* 'a hedgehog'; *neither to hup nor wynd* 'move neither to the left or right', 'prove obstinate'. It could be argued, of course, that some of these words are specific to agriculture and might well be known by (older) speakers in the farming community; so too some of the words cited may now simply be obsolete. But it does seem to be the case that while Scots dictionaries can list tens of thousands of words alleged to be uniquely Scots, not all of them are necessarily known to the majority of current speakers of the language.

Many words are, however, instantly recognisable as Scots: *kirk, minister, first-foot, whisky, haggis, tartan* and *Hogmanay*. Also among this overtly Scots group could be included items like *aye* 'yes', *ken* 'know', *gey* 'very' and *dram* 'a whisky measure'. However, there are others which, although their meaning is familiar to most Modern Scots speakers, may well be used by Standard English speakers unaware that they are Scottish in origin: *bramble, burn* 'a stream'; *infirmary, jaggy, rowan*, and perhaps even *hoist* 'elevator/lift'. But there are also very many other words which, although their meanings may be known to particular groups in society (older people, regional dialect speakers and agricultural workers, for example), have a very limited currency among Scots speakers at large and whose meaning may well be unknown to them. Among this group are words such as *bauchle* 'an untidy person', *capoosh* 'a hood', *carsackie* 'an overall', *dowf* 'dull', *faugh* 'pale', *fauld* 'a sheep pen', *hilch* 'a limp', *pauchle* 'to shuffle', *skaup* 'the skull' and many others. At the same time, there is a kind of 'intermediate' group of words which, although containing many words which are recognisably Scots, are probably in wider general currency: *wheen* 'many', *boke* 'to vomit', *cowp* 'to topple over', *glaikit* 'stupid', *scunner* 'to disgust', *oxter* 'armpit', *stoor* 'dust' and *fash* 'to upset'.

In the 1980s a very interesting study was carried out in the New Town of Livingston (Pollner:1980) to determine to what extent speakers were able to comprehend the meaning of a wide range of Scots vocabulary and to see whether such knowledge co-related to the speaker's age or social class. Pollner looked at a set of nine schoolchildren, aged around 13, and a larger set of adults between 25 and 50 years of age (so no elderly informants were sampled). Pollner selected three groups of Scots vocabulary items, ranging from those which were 'very Scots' (and might be expected to be understood by relatively few of the informants) to those which (although obviously Scots) had a rather wider currency in the community. In the first group were words like *biel* 'to shelter'; *cuit* 'ankle'; *grosser* 'gooseberry'; *guttie stick* 'forked stick'; *spirtle* 'stick for stirring porridge'; *stirk* 'bullock'; *skelf* 'small piece of wood lodged under the skin'. The second group contained Scots words with a very wide distribution throughout the Lowland area, words such as *bairn*; *chiel*; *darg* 'task'; *dreich* 'wet, miserable'; *siller* 'silver, money'; *stour* 'dirt'; and *wean* 'child'. A third group contained 'Scots' words which have an even wider, non-local currency and which even appear in major English-language dictionaries such as *Longman's Dictionary of Contemporary English*, words like *ken* 'to know'; *pinkie* 'little finger'; and *wee* 'small'.

A

B

I disagree. A words are well-known
B words are not.

34

Although the results were complex, Pollner showed that the age and social class of the speakers were vitally important factors in meaning recognition. The sex of the informants, on the other hand, had no statistical significance at all. The adult group showed an almost fifty percent knowledge of the meanings of all types of words selected, while only around a quarter of the children performed well. Both children and adults showed more than a fifty percent rate of familiarity with words like *bairn, ken, pinkie, skelf, wean* and *wee* (i.e. of words which appear in general dictionaries). Fewer than fifty percent of the adults knew words which were perceived as having a fairly wide distribution throughout Lowland Scotland – words such as *chiel, sheuch, siller, spirtle*. On the other hand, none of the children recognised any of these words. Indeed, neither children nor adults recognised the meanings of the kinds of words which were 'very Scots' – words which appear in specialised Scots dictionaries – words like *biel, crit, darg grosser, guttie stick* and *skeelie*.

An interesting fact emerged from this study concerning the relationship between social class and knowledge of the meanings of Scots vocabulary items. While there was a fairly even overall percentage recognition by both Working Class and Middle Class speakers (around forty percent recognition), there was much variation with respect to individual words. For example, 24% Middle Class speakers recognised *chiel* as against 16% Working Class; 20% Middle Class recognition of *sheuch* against only 3% Working Class. While there was 36% recognition of *trauchle* among Middle Class speakers, there was a 48% recognition of the item among Working Class speakers. Pollner suggested that perhaps Middle Class enhanced recognition of 'broad' Scots words resulted from their reading of and greater familiarity with Scottish literary texts where such vocabulary might regularly appear.

4.2. Meaning Structures

Individual words obviously have a semantic meaning: 'car', 'horse', 'cathedral' and 'happiness' are items to which we can attach either a physical or intellectual co-relation in the real world. At the same time, it is possible for individual words to combine in a way which enhances or expands the meaning of their individual components: words such as 'blackboard', 'White House' and even a combination of words like 'Weetabix' ('wheat', 'and', 'biscuits'). Each of the components of these words – 'black', 'board' – is itself indivisible without having an effect which will destroy its meaning: we cannot meaningfully break down 'black' into 'bl' and 'ack' and in any way preserve the original concept the word denoted. The indivisible and meaning-bearing components of words are known as **morphemes**. Thus 'blackbird' is made up of two morphemes, while 'bird' is a single morpheme (and a single word).

However, a language like English has the ability to produce words made up of several morphemes, some of which cannot usually stand on their own and make meaningful sense. Consider a word like 'unmentionable'. Clearly we have here a word which has a 'core' or 'root' morpheme which is modified by other elements like 'un' and 'able' which, although meaningful, do not usually stand on their own as words (we do not usually say 'an un' or 'the able'). In other words, an item like 'unmentionable' has an internal meaning structure which we might characterise as:

$$[_1 \text{un } [_2 [_3 \text{mention}_3] \text{ able}_2] \ _1]$$

Although they do not usually 'stand on their own' as individual words, both 'un' and 'able' have recognisable meanings – 'not' and 'capable of being' – meanings which can be equally well used with other 'core' morphemes as in 'unconscious' and 'treatable' and so on. Words like 'thoughtlessness' and 'restlessness' show a similar complex meaning structure, with nouns like 'thought' and 'rest' showing the addition of **suffixes** 'less' and 'ness'. The former suffix adds the concept of negativity, while the latter – the 'ness' – performs a **grammatical** function by changing what is an adjective 'thoughtless' into a noun. Such morphemes added to the end of base components often modify or add to the meaning of the base morpheme itself, thus contrasts like 'lion/lioness'; 'star/starlet'. Meaningful components attached to the left-hand side of the root morpheme (often called **prefixes**) – the 'in' of 'indescribable' – are usually meaning bearing. Thus affixes like 'un' in 'unappealing', 'anti' in 'anticlimax, 'super' in 'superhuman', 're' in 'reapply' and 'co' in 'cohabit' can be said to modify the meaning of the base component in the compound morpheme in a variety of different ways.

However, as we have seen, suffixes in particular can perform a purely grammatical role in that they can change one part of speech into another – nouns and adjectives into verbs ('orchestrate'; 'deafen'; 'advertise'); concrete nouns into abstract nouns ('mile'/'mileage'; 'friend'/'friendship'); adjectives into adverbs ('quick/quickly'; 'sudden/suddenly'); nouns from verbs ('speaker/ speak'; 'rider/ride'); adjectives from nouns ('socialist/social'; 'capitalist/capital'); and adjectives from verbs ('like/likeable'; 'drink/drinkable'), among others. However, but only very occasionally, prefixes can have a grammatical function as well – the change of noun to verb in 'friend/befriend', 'rage/enrage' and 'compass'/encompass'). The general name given to this type of grammatical role morphology is **derivational morphology**.

The vocabulary of many non-standard varieties of Modern Scots contains many words composed of 'core' components modified by prefixes and suffixes. One of the most common of these is the prefix 'mis-', usually imparting a negative meaning to the core component in the word, thus: *mislikely* 'to make unlikely', *misliken* 'to speak ill of', *misdoubt* 'to distrust'; *mishanter* 'misfortune'. With a negative implication too we find the prefix 'wan' in combinations like: *wanchance, wanluck* 'misfortune', *wanwordy* 'unworthy', *wangrace* 'bad behaviour'; *wanworth* 'worthless'. Somewhat less common are words with prefixes beginning with *cur* and *ram*, a specific meaning for which is difficult to define. Some examples are *curcuddoch* 'good humoured'; *curmurring* 'low rumbling; the purring of a cat'; *curmud* 'close', 'intimate'; *ramfeezle* 'to confuse'; *rambust* 'robust'; *ramstoorie* 'rough', where the *ram* prefix is perhaps related to the noun *ramie* 'a free for all'.

Suffixes in Modern Scots are perhaps more plentiful in the language's morphology and their function perhaps more clear.

For instance, the 'ie' or 'y' suffixes are often used for the purpose of forming adjectives and nouns from other parts of speech. Thus, we find *gemmie* 'somebody who is game'; *batchie* 'a baker'; *stushie* 'an uproar'; *steamie* 'a communal washhouse'; *riddie* 'a red face, a blush', likewise *kiltie* 'a highlander'; *cludgie* 'a toilet'. In adjective formation we find: *goskie* 'luxuriant' (from the noun *gosk* 'coarse grass'); *couthgie* 'well liked, agreeable'; *grippie* 'greedy'. This suffix is used too to form diminutives as in: *wifie*, *lassie*, *laddie* and *sweetie*. Sometimes this same suffix appears in combination with another Scots diminutive suffix in '-ock', to form double diminutives: *wifockie*, *lassockie*. The *ock* suffix on its own is still quite common, as in: *winnock* 'small window'; *lassock* 'little lass'; *whilock* 'a little while' and even as an affection or familiarity marker with personal names: *Jimmock* 'Jimmy'; *Sannock* 'Sandy', *Kittock* 'Kitty' and *Bessock* 'Betsy'. Less common now in everyday usage is the suffix *rife*, indicating concepts like 'liable to be', 'able to be', 'having a tendency to', thus: *salerife* 'saleable'; *wildrife* 'disposed to be wild'; *waukrife* 'wakeful'; *mockrife* 'mocking'.

The Standard English '-ish' suffix denoting degree, as in 'blackish', 'yellowish' and 'nearish' is often manifested in non-standard Scots by 'like' or even (but perhaps recessively now) 'kind', thus *blacklike*, *doucelike*, *siccan* (contraction of 'such kind') and *whaten* (a contraction of 'what-kind').

4.3. Word Formation

English – not unlike German – has had considerable success in increasing its stock of words by the device of combining existing words in several different ways, called **compounding**. Some of the more exotic of these combinations are to be found in advertising contexts:

Lipsmackinthirstquenschinacetastinmotivatingoodbuzzincool talkinhighwalkinfastlivinnevergivincoolfizzin – PEPSI,

where we see a single adjective built from a succession of individual adjectival units. Again *Guintelligence Test,* a combination of *Guinness* and *Intelligence* or *Schweppervescence,* a combination of *Schweppes* and *effervescence*. Such compounds (sometimes known also as *blends*) are common in everyday English as well, and include items such as *breathalyser*, *Oxbridge*, *smog* (*smoke+fog*), *motel* (*motor+hotel*) and many others. More common, perhaps, are compounds involving the bringing together of two root morphemes: *blackbird*, *gunboat*, *businessman*, *redcoat*, *cowboy*, *steamboat*, although the grammatical relationship which exists between the two components of the compound is not always the same.

Compounding is also a common characteristic of Modern Scots and can take a number of different forms. Perhaps the most common is the compounding of an initial prepositional word (often denoting a spacial characteristic), thus: *owercoup* 'overthrow'; *ootding* 'drive out, expel'; *owerturn*; *owerhye*; *uppit* 'put up'; *uplook*; *upget*; *upgive*; *upstuck*; *ootcast*; *ootby*. The item *sweetie* is much favoured in compounding, thus: *sweetie-boolie* 'a round, boiled sweet'; *sweetie bottle* 'a glass jar for holding sweets'; sw*eetie-man* 'confectioner'; *sweetie-shop*; *sweetie-wife* 'a female sweet seller' or, perhaps more commonly now, 'a gossipy (?male) person'. *Hen* is also used as a compound word and phrase-forming item (although perhaps less commonly than *sweetie*) as in: *hen-hertit* 'chicken hearted'; *hen-taed* 'hen toed or pigeon toed'; *hen-plooks* 'goose flesh'; *hen-wife* 'a poultry woman' or, perhaps more usually now, 'a male who concerns himself with female matters'.

Miscellaneous compounds include: *midgie-raker*; *midgie-bin*; *midgie-man* where *midgie* is the Scots for 'midden' or 'refuse'; *bidie-in* 'an unmarried live-in partner'; *chanty-wrestler* 'a chancer' (?'a chamber-pot wrestler'!); *sodie-heid* 'featherbrained'.

New words can be formed too by shortening or **clipping** existing morphemes, thus in Standard English: *bus* (for 'omnibus'); *piano* ('pianoforte'); *porn* ('pornography'); *fridge* ('refrigerator'), *sitcom* ('situation comedy'). Clipping can occur through deleting a syllable from either the front of the word (**front-clipping**: *bus*), the rear of the word (**back-clipping**: *piano*) or from both: (*fridge*). Front clipping examples from Modern Scots might include: *fend* 'to defend'; *guise* ' to disguise'; *mineer* 'domineer'; *maist* 'almost'. On the other hand, instances such as: *photie* 'photograph'; *scaffie* 'a street cleaner', 'scavenger'; *bookie* 'bookmaker'; *Hibees* 'Hibernian'; and *sannies* 'sandshoes' show back clipping. Front and back clipped items are: *Weegie* 'Glaswegian'; *Piskie* 'Episcopalian'; *Proddie* 'Protestant' and *tattie* 'potato' + the *ie* suffix.

Additional vocabulary items have been achieved in Standard English by naming objects or conditions employing the names of those individuals perceived to have been associated with them (**eponyms**), thus: *sandwich*; *wellington*; *dunce* (Duns Scotus, the medieval Scottish theologian); *Stetson* (John B. Stetson, the nineteenth-century US hatmaker); *balaclava*. This process is common in Modern Scots as well, where we see: *Jessie*; *Jimmy*; *Teenie* (generic names for females, males and small children); *klondyker* (factory ship for fish processing); and *paisley* (pattern). Here too we can consider *rab ha* (the general name given to gluttons after the nineteenth-century Glasgow glutton Robert Hall); *tam o'shanter* (a type of bonnet); *Glasgow screwdriver* (a strong drink); a *shankie* (a lavatory, after the Barrhead maker of lavatories – Shanks).

Modern Scots can manipulate the vocabulary of Standard English through changes to the grammatical function of individual items. For instance, words which are mainly treated as nouns in Standard English can be used as (a) verbs: *to college* 'to educate at university'; *to plank* 'to hide'; *to mind* 'to remember'; (b) as adjectives: *gallus* 'wild, impudent, gritty' possibly from 'gallows'. In the same way, adjectives in the Standard language can be used as nouns in Scots, thus *Hairy* 'a low class woman' (*a wee hairy*), and verbs can be used as nouns: *a differ* 'a difference'; *a dine* 'dinner'; *a dare* 'he did it for a dare'.

4.4. *Scots Vocabulary from Foreign Sources*

In common with many European languages, English has seen many additions to its native vocabulary stock as a result of contact with other languages and cultures. The language is replete with borrowed items from many non-English sources, acquisitions which result from invasion (Norman French and Scandinavian words), cultural contact (French, Latin and

Greek words) and exploration and Empire-building (North American, Indian and Malaysian indigenous languages among many others). These innovations have occurred at every period in the language's history and are ongoing (although today most borrowings are from other regional types of English – notably United States English and Australian English). However, it should be noted that this kind of process is often regarded with concern among language purists, and steps are sometimes taken at the highest governmental levels to discourage the use of vocabulary from other languages. Such is the case today in France, Russia, Japan and parts of French-speaking Canada where there is official discouragement of the adoption of English vocabulary. The extent of borrowing is, of course, very closely tied to the function language is being used for, English words being extremely common, for instance, in scientific and technical journals written in Japanese and Russian.

The English used in Scotland too has seen considerable foreign addition to its native, core vocabulary at all periods in its history and from a diverse range of sources. In the fifteenth and sixteenth centuries, principally as a result of substantial cultural contact with **France**, there were several (many long-lasting) additions to the language's word-stock. Notable among these are *gardyloo* 'toilet'; *Hogmanay* 'New Year's Eve' (reputedly from Northern French *houginane* 'a gift given on New Year's Eve'); *fash* 'to annoy oneself' (French *fâcher*); *dour* 'miserable' (Fr *dur* 'hard'); *ashet* 'an oval serving plate' (French *assiette*); *corbie* 'raven' (Old French *corbe*). At this period too from French are: *visage*, *plesant*, *tendir*, *noble*, *countenance*, *redolent*, *disjune* 'breakfast', *cummer* 'female crony' and many others. In more recent times, French loan words into Scots include: *howtowdie* 'young chicken for cooking' (early French *hétoudeau*), *cartoush* 'a woman's short jacket' (French *court* + *housse* 'a short coarse garment') and *biggin* 'a linen cap' (French *béguin* 'a cap').

Scandinavian (Danish and Norwegian) settlement in Scotland in the ninth and tenth centuries (and until more recent times in the Northern Isles) has meant that there are considerable numbers of words which have been introduced into the Scots (and indeed general English) word-stock from these sources. Appearing in Scots at an early date are words like: *tyke* 'cur'; *to flit* 'move house'; *brae* 'hill'; *lass* 'young woman'; *skelp* 'to slap'; *birk* 'birch'; *muckle* 'much/great'; *maun* 'must'; *kirk* 'church'; *lowp* 'leap'; *kist* 'chest'; *gowk* 'a fool' (Norse *gaukr*); and *lug* 'ear'. More recent additions from the eighteenth and nineteenth centuries onwards are, in the main, confined to those dialect areas where Scandinavian influence (in particular Norwegian) was most profound and long-lasting, notably in Caithness, Orkney and Shetland: *gizzen* 'to shrink' (Norwegian *gissen*); *brainyell* 'to rush out' (Norwegian *brengja*); *cleester* 'to plaster' (Danish *klistre*); *fuggle* 'a small bundle of hay' (Norwegian *fugge*); *floan* 'woman who shows affection to men in an inappropriate way' (Norwegian *flana*), among many others.

Cultural and trading links between Scotland and the Low Countries have always been (and continue to be) strong. Consequently there are a great many items of Scots (and general English) vocabulary which originate from **Dutch** and **Flemish** sources. Words such as *rumple* 'to crease'; *howff* ('a pub' but originally 'a courtyard' or even 'a burial ground'); *smoor* 'to suffocate'; *keek* 'to glance'; and *scone*. Many of the borrowed words have to do with trade and industry, and are to be found in Scots from medieval times. Among these are *callant* 'customer' (now 'a young man'); *coft* 'bought'; and *kinkin* 'a quarter barrel'. Yet there are also many words relating to more general matters such as *sweinger* 'a scoundrel'; *rumple* 'to crease or wrinkle'; *doup* 'backside' (originally 'bottom of an eggshell'); *bum* 'backside'; *cuit* 'ankle'; *dok* 'backside'; *swanky* 'smart'; *golf*; and *pinkie*.

Unsurprisingly, there are many areas of the vocabulary of both early and Modern Scots where the influence of the word-stock of **Scottish Gaelic** is strong. From this source and at a very early period were taken words referring to geophysical features such as: *bog, cairn, inch* 'an island', *glen, loch, craig, strath, corrie* and *ben*. Early period borrowings include too: *sonsie* 'lucky, friendly', now 'attractive, good looking'; *ingill* 'domestic fire(place)'; *bladdoch* 'buttermilk'; *car* (*corrie*) fisted 'left hand'; *messan* 'small pet dog'; *capercaille* 'wood grouse';

slogan 'war cry'; *clan; clarsach* 'Highland harp'. Other, still common, early borrowings are: *tocher* 'dowry'; *whisky; dochandorus* 'drinking cup'; and *bard*.

More recently from this source we have *kelpie* 'water demon'; *crannog* 'wooden settlement in loch'; *Sassenach* 'English person or Lowlander'; *trews* 'tartan trousers'; *sgiandubh* 'ornamental dagger'; *fillebeg* 'little kilt'; *sporran* 'purse'; *claymore* 'sword'; *quaich* 'shallow drinking cup'; *mod* 'assembly'; *ceilidh* 'evening singing party'; *keelie* 'urban dweller'. Less-used Gaelic borrowings in the modern period also include words like: *coachie* 'soft'; *drollan* 'half-wit'; *oorcan* 'bunion'; *mirkie* 'cheerful'; *dornack* 'something large'; *glormach* 'garish'; *garlach* 'a rascal'; *smiach* 'a whisper'; *juskal* 'old'; *stripach* 'harlot'; *loogan* 'rogue'; *mirran* 'a carrot'.

In common with most varieties of English, Scots has a large contingent of words which derive from classical sources, notably **Latin**. Such words are often most obviously to be found in specialised cultural and social contexts, most especially in the areas of law, education and the church. Scots law terminology such as *cessio honorum, delectus personae, nobile officium,* and *locus* ('site of a crime') is to be widely found in written documents as well as in the spoken language at the Bar. Education-related vocabulary such as *dominie* 'school master'; *dux* 'school medalist'; *palmie* and *pandie* 'to cane on the hand'; *fugie* 'to play truant'; and *quaestor/servitor/janitor* all have Latin sources. Although most of the vocabulary is now obsolete, there was a huge influx of Latinate vocabulary into Scottish literary writing in the sixteenth century, especially in the aureate diction of what are known as the Scottish Chaucerians (notably Henryson and Dunbar). Words of Latin origin in their works include: *eterne* 'eternal'; *discerne; angelicall; matern* 'mother'; *dispone* 'dispose'; *disperne* 'disperse'; *hodiern* 'daily'; *sempiter,* 'eternal', among many others.

[handwritten: Xoh dear! Who spelt this thus?]

Suggested Reading

Munro, M. 1985. *The Patter: A Guide to Current Glasgow Usage.* Glasgow.

Murison, D.D. 1971. 'The Dutch element in the vocabulary of Scots', in Aitken, A.J., McIntosh, A. and Palsson, H. eds. *Edinburgh Studies in English and Scots.* London. Longman, pp. 159–176.

*Pollner, C. 1985. 'Old words in a young town'. *Scottish Language* 4, pp. 5–15.

*Robinson, M. 1985. ed. *The Concise Scots Dictionary.* Aberdeen. Aberdeen University Press.

*Stevenson, J.A.C. 1989. *Scoor-oot. A Dictionary of Scots Words and Phrases in Current Use.* London.

CHAPTER FIVE

Language in Modern Scottish Society

5.1. Social Variation

There are at least two characteristics of language with which nearly all speakers are familiar and upon which they will be prepared to comment (and even pontificate). One of these is the way in which language is perceived as serving as a means of expressing group identity in the broadest sense. Many speakers are proud of the way they speak – seeing in it a reflection of where they come from and as an identifying mark of the social group with which they most closely identify or wish to identify. At the same time, speakers are often prepared to be quite judgmental about the ways in which other people use language. Although on occasion they will comment on the pure or refined characteristics of other people's speech ('cut glass vowels' somehow always attract attention), most often they will make an outright condemnation of the speech of their fellow citizens as being vulgar, ugly, slovenly, lazy, incorrect or uneducated, condemning 'strangulated vowels' and 'nasalised twangs'. Even highly educated individuals are capable of being negatively judgmental in this way, as the following observation by a Glasgow University lecturer on the speech habits of working-class citizens in the city shows (Macaulay and Trevelyan: 1977:137): 'The accent of the lowest state of Glaswegians is the ugliest accent one can encounter, but that is partly because it is associated with the unwashed and the violent'.

In other circumstances individuals will often equally vehemently deride the speech habits of those in those social groups they perceive to be more prestigious, calling them posh, affected, showing off, putting on airs and graces or even speaking with a mouthful of marbles (*jorries*)! At the same time speakers will openly defend their linguistic habits even when these are generally regarded as having a low prestige by other members of society. See how a Working Class adult reacted when asked whether it would be advantageous to change his accent when being interviewed for a job (Macaulay and Trevelyan: 1977:137): 'Well, a lot of people don't like the Glasgow dialect, the way I'm speaking just now, you see they don't like that at all, that's not proper English. This is the way we have always spoken'.

Another lower Middle Class 15-year-old Glaswegian commented, when asked whether it would be better to sound like an Englishman when being interviewed for a job (Macaulay and Trevelyan: 1977:132): 'I don't know that I would. I wouldn't like to have an English accent. I think it is a very daft one. They pronounce words correctly but they don't sound very nice. In your own environment you'd feel out of place. If you live in Glasgow you must talk like a Glaswegian, but not to the extent of broad Glasgow'.

Notice that while this last speaker is conscious of the possible inappropriateness of using a more acceptable regional or social dialect in a Glaswegian context, he nevertheless emphasises the importance of avoiding certain non-prestigious Glasgow usage. Yet there appears to be for many speakers an overriding sense that the language they use in everyday situations is a cause for embarrassment, coupled with a sense of admiration (?) for (in particular) the sound of the standard:

It's a wee bit difficult for me with ma history and background and the way Ah speak, you see, tae change it to speak to you if Ah met you just along the road. It's a wee bit of a struggle Ah would say...well, for me tae speak. Ah would be afraid that Ah might've used the wrong grammar and sayed the wrong words, so this kept me quiet for a wee bit, ye know? It was ... lots i times Ah felt like speaking at the meetings, but Ah was afraid because of the – hearing how Ah – Ah like tae hear their accents, the other members – how Ah thought – an it was – they weren't – it was just easy for them tae speak; they weren't puttin anything on; they were just speakin just naturally proper. But I enjoyed listenin tae them, and I used tae wonder how tae phrase ma questions an how tae speak (Macafee 1983:23).

Such subjective views are not, of course, confined to urban Central Belt usage and there is a view that while accents like those of Glasgow or Dundee are in some way stigmatised, those of Inverness and the English spoken in the Highlands are pleasing, 'lilting' and the like. Yet it is interesting to observe the result of a UK national poll recently held by British Telecom. People were asked their view of what they considered to be the most pleasing British English accents used in Call Centres. The Glasgow accent (especially when delivered by a female voice) came top of the poll. Clearly, such normative views of certain Scottish English accents have important repercussions in the classroom context; teachers have a difficult set of decisions to make as to how to deal with linguistic prejudice and preconception affecting the language children (particularly Working Class children) bring to the classroom from the home.

Like every other form of spoken language, the English used in Scotland is subject to change, even very short-term change. Much of that change is driven by factors which fall outside language proper and belong to the social domain. For instance, speakers of English can produce two kinds of [l] sound: one in a word like *mill*, the other in a word like *Mull*. In the former, the tip of the tongue touches the roof of the mouth at the front, while in the other it does so further back on the roof of the mouth. These are sometimes respectively known as clear and dark [l] sounds and are represented in the phonetic alphabet by the symbols [l] and [ł]. The appearance of one or the other is totally predictable: the front vowel of *mill* selects the front [l], the back vowel of *Mull* the back, dark [ł]. The speaker makes the choice automatically, as it were. However, in some groups of speakers, the dark [ł] has come to be used in both contexts. In Edinburgh, for example, this occurs very noticeably among Working Class male speakers, giving the use of the dark [ł] a social value of which many of the speakers in this group are conscious – especially female Working Class speakers. When these women are in social situations where they are conscious that their use of language is being monitored (say when they are asked to read something aloud), it is noticeable that they tend to shy away from the dark [ɫ] form, preferring to use the light front [l] since it does not have the same Working Class and male associations. In such a case the selection of the pronunciation of [l] is not automatically determined by the surrounding sounds, but by extra-linguistic, social considerations – in this case the desire to avoid what are held by women to be stigmatised *male* Working Class pronunciations.

5.2. Sex, social class and situation

Although there are almost certainly many more, three main extra-linguistic factors appear to determine the kind of language speakers use: these are **gender**, **social class**, and **consciousness of being linguistically observed by others**. Indeed, all three factors normally interact and none is by itself wholly definitive, although gender may have an especially important role to play. In many (especially Western) societies speakers will produce certain types of language according to the ways in which they identify themselves (or are seen as others as identified) with a particular social class or division. **Social class** can, of course, be based on a wide range of criteria: educational attainment, type of occupation, level of wage/salary and area of residence, among other identifying characteristics. The customary and rather crude division often made in this area is between Upper Middle Class, Lower Middle Class and Working Class usage. Very tentatively, we might characterise these social groups according to occupational criteria. Employers, managers, professionals, own account workers, administrators, what are often referred to as 'white collar workers', might be considered as Upper Middle Class. Those working in the service industries, offering a personal service, foremen and supervisors as well as skilled manual workers, may be classified as Lower Middle Class (known as 'blue collar').

Semi-skilled and unskilled manual workers and, perhaps, agricultural workers might be considered as members of the Working Class. None of these socio-economic divisions is entirely reliable as an indicator of social class, and many other factors come into play. But we shall use social class terminology in this chapter in this relatively crude fashion.

The **consciousness of being linguistically observed by others** very often corresponds to the **level of formality** in the context where the speech event takes place. In other words, the extent to which a speaker is conscious of being observed by others for the way he or she speaks can play an important role in the kind of language an individual is likely to use. To assess their reaction to awareness levels, speakers are observed in different types of situation in which the speech act takes place:

(a) when reading pairs of words and lists of words (i.e. when speakers know they are being tested for their linguistic habits and even for which ones);

(b) in relatively informal (often group) interview situations when speakers may only be indirectly aware of being observed;

(c) when speakers are completely unaware that they are being observed (surreptitiously recorded spontaneous conversation).

When speech is measured against criteria like these, a classic pattern (sometimes known as the **Labovian paradigm**) emerges:

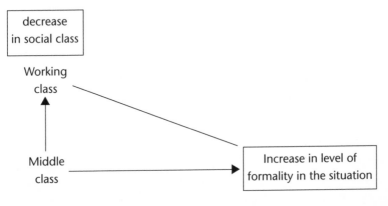

The height of the diagonal line represents the frequency of stigmatised or 'vulgar', non-standard forms. The direction of the diagonal line clearly shows that such stigmatised, or vulgar, forms – not surprisingly – *increase* with a lowering both of the social class of the informant and *decrease* with a heightening of formality in the linguistic situation or context. In other words, Working Class speakers tend in general to use more stigmatised forms than do Middle Class speakers, and both social groups use more non-standard forms when they are least conscious of being listened to than they do when they are reading lists of words. Increasing the level of formality in the situation and/or increasing the social class of the speaker *serves to diminish the use of non-standard forms.*

For example, the following chart shows what has been found to be the prevalence of glottal stop substitution for [t] – in words like 'water' [waʔɅr], 'hit it' [hɪʔ ɪʔ] – mapped against social class categories among speakers in Glasgow and Edinburgh. The frequency of the stigmatised glottal stop is high among Working Class speakers (especially when speaking in informal contexts), lower among Lower Middle Class speakers and lower still among Upper Middle Class speakers: see Figure 5.1.

However, we need to qualify such an obvious conclusion. There are no speakers in any social class whose language is

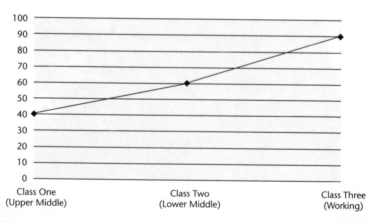

Figure 5.1. Frequency of glottal stop for [t] in Glasgow and Edinburgh speakers: mapped against social class.

homogeneous. All Middle Class speakers can show glottalisation of voiceless [t]; indeed, the evidence from several surveys – including those of Glasgow and Edinburgh – shows glottalisation spreading to the Middle Classes from the Working Class – what is known as a **'change from below'** characteristic; that is, innovations are spreading from lower-class speakers to those in the social class above, not – as used to be thought – the other way around, the 'good' speech of the Middle Class being 'copied' by speakers in lower socio-economic groups. Again, Working Class speakers themselves (especially female speakers) can show a reluctance to use stigmatised forms like glottals in those situations where they are conscious that others are paying attention to the way they speak (as when they are reading aloud, for example). But it is most important to stress how Figure 5.1 clearly shows the extent to which this apparently stigmatised pronunciation is a feature of the speech of Middle Class speakers and is not confined to the Working Class. It would seem that the stigmatised form is being accepted (perhaps subconsciously) by the Middle Class speaker and that a language change is taking place such that a socially 'lower' class form is moving into the social class above.

A good example of the inter-connection between the use of language and the social class and, in this instance, the sex of the speaker in Scotland can be found by looking at the ways in which sentences involving **modal verbs** like *can, will, would* as well as the verb *to be* come to be **negated** [see §2.2.2, §2.2.3]. Standard Scottish English speakers will produce contrasts like 'I will go/I will not go/I won't go'; 'I can go/I can not go/I can't go'; 'she is ready/she is not ready/she isn't ready' and so on. Notice how there are two processes involved here: the first simply involves placing the negative word 'not' immediately following the (modal) verb – 'I can go/I can not go', while the other involves the attachment of the negative word as if it were *inside* the verb – thus 'I can't go'. This process is called **cliticisation** and can be found in several contexts in Modern English: compare the sentence 'Drink a pint of milk a day' with its equivalent in the advertising slogan 'Drinka pinta milka day'. In the last instance the indefinite articles 'a', normally in construction with the noun to their right, have come to be attached to the verb and noun preceding them. The speaker interprets the indefinite articles as an integral part of the nouns to their left. This has occurred to such an extent that we can even have 'one pinta' and 'two pintas'. Likewise phrases like 'got to', 'want to' have cliticised versions in 'gotta' and 'wanna'.

In the case of the Scots negative modals and the verb 'to be' we can also find cliticised versions such as 'I willnae', 'I cannae' and 'he isnae'. Recent sociolinguistic studies of Edinburgh and Ayr have shown the extent to which the occurrence of the cliticised 'nae' forms is closely tied to the social class and the sex of the speaker. For example, in Edinburgh it is only the Working Class speaker who will use the 'cannae' and 'willnae' types. Even in interview situations where the informants were conscious of being recorded, there was still a high incidence of these forms for Working Class speakers in general. Nevertheless, these speakers are very conscious of the negative social value of these forms, since their occurrence does decrease the more formal the context becomes. However, the form is especially sensitive to the sex of the speaker. Although female Working Class speakers do use 'isnae', 'cannae' cliticised forms, they do so much less frequently than the males in their group, preferring 'won't' and 'can't' types.

Interestingly, in Edinburgh there seems to be a clear tendency for the clitic versions to be used more widely among *young* Working Class speakers than those of the older generation – the vernacular, stigmatised form is spreading among this young group. However, there is no indication at all that this kind of usage is spreading to the Middle Classes. While there is evidence to show that changes can spread from a lower to a higher social class – as we have just seen in the case of the glottal stop – the use of the cliticised negatives does not fall into this pattern. Forms like 'isnae', 'willnae' and the like are clearly too saliently marked for Working Class status for their use to spread into Middle Class communities. That is, the Middle Class speaker has a different level of consciousness of the social value of the '–nae' negatives than he/she does of (the equally Working Class prominent) glottal stop. For the Working Class young male, however, the 'willnae', 'disnae' forms have a macho, rough, streetwise appeal and are therefore spreading throughout that particular group.

The speaker's **gender** plays a very significant role in the selection of linguistic forms (particularly, but not exclusively, in pronunciation) in Modern Scots. Two instances are observable where it is primarily the gender of the speaker which determines the selection of a particular pronunciation type. Consider, in the first place, the ways in which the sound [r] is pronounced in Edinburgh. There seem to be at least two different kinds of [r]-sound in the city. One type involves the tongue making a quick tap against the front upper teeth or the ridge immediately behind them – the symbol for this sound being [r]. The second is not unlike the sound United States English speakers use for the final sound in words like 'far', 'car' – there is only a little contact between the tongue and any part of the teeth or palate and the sound is voiced: the symbol for this sound (technically known as a *voiced continuant frictionless approximant*) is [ɹ]. The distribution of the tap versus the approximant [r]-sound is very much a function of the gender of Edinburgh speakers. While there is also a strong class-tie – the tap associated with Working Class, the approximant with Middle Class – there is much evidence to suggest that the approximant [ɹ] is coming to be used as the preferred form of the syllable final [r]-sound, in words like 'tar', 'far', 'bar', with *females* throughout the city. In particular, young Edinburgh females of Working Class status are starting to adopt this [ɹ] which, for their mothers' generation, was a predominantly Middle Class sound. On the other hand, there seems to be little shift in the direction of the [ɹ] variant among male speakers in any social class. Indeed, there is a form of the [r]-sound which is favoured predominantly by the Working Class male in the city (and perhaps in Glasgow too). This is what is known as the pharyngealised [r]-sound, where the tongue root is drawn to the back wall of the throat (the pharynx), giving the sound a dark quality – indeed sounding as if the speaker were being strangled! The symbol for this sound is [ʕ]. It can be heard very clearly in the Working Class male valedictory 'Cheers!' – [ʧiʌʕz], as well as in words like 'here' [hiʌʕ] and [ðɛʌʕ] 'there'.

But it is perhaps the manifestations of the vowel which appears in words like 'cat', 'sat' and 'mat' which are the most revealing when we look at gender and class usage in Edinburgh. In the high prestige areas of the city – for instance Morningside – it is still common to hear Middle Class women over fifty years of age using a raised vowel like [ɛ] (as in a word like 'get' or 'set') in words of this kind. There is, in effect, for these speakers a merger between 'pat' and 'pet' words. However, an interesting sociological factor comes into play – the Morningside dialect is seen as almost stereotypically posh in the city: Working Class speakers will often ridicule it through imitation, indeed often caricaturing it by pronouncing a word like 'sacks' as if it were 'sex'. This view of the Middle Class pronunciation as a **class stereotype** appears to affect the usage of *younger* Middle Class females to the extent that they apparently quite consciously avoid [sɛks] for 'sacks' and [pɛt] for 'pat', abandoning the [ɛ] vowel of the older Middle Class female generation for the Standard Scottish English [a].

This phenomenon, which we might call **stereotype-avoidance**, is also to be found among Working Class women in the city. Working Class *male* speakers quite consistently use a lower and further back vowel in words like 'cat' and 'pat' – a vowel not unlike that found in Standard English in words like 'bath', 'after' and 'class' – the [ɑ] vowel. In Working Class communities in Edinburgh this vowel appears to be as significant a marker for maleness as the [ɛ] vowel in 'pat' is one for age and gender among the Middle Class Morningside speakers. For example, Working Class male speakers will tend not to avoid the low back vowel, even in those contexts (for example reading lists of words) where they are very conscious that their accent is being listened to. Indeed, there is some evidence to suggest that they even exaggerate the use of this vowel in such contexts as an overt signal of their gender and class tie. Interestingly, however, Working Class women seem to recognise this vowel as a sign of overt masculinity, and avoid its use, replacing the [ɑ] vowel with the low front [a] (as in Standard Scottish English 'cat'). In this way, it appears that females in Edinburgh of both the Middle and the Working Classes are, for reasons of stereotype-avoidance (one in reaction to the high prestige Morningside, the other to the male Working Class pronunciation) coming to use the same [a] vowel in 'cat' and 'sat' type words.

5.3. Ongoing Change and Dialect Levelling

Social status identification through language can involve two apparently contradictory factors. On the one hand, speakers can change their language in the direction of what they consider to be a more prestigious type in their local community, or even in a wider, national, context. A good example of this is the way in which many Middle Class Scottish speakers will use diphthongs like [eɪ] and [oʊ] in words like 'say' and 'go' (normally monophthongal [se] and [go] in Scottish Standard English) apparently in an attempt to produce what is perceived as a highly prestigious Standard English Middle Class usage. Again, TV and radio presenters (particularly females) will tend to use the Standard English low back vowel [ɑ] – in words like 'Glasgow' and 'father' – rather than the Scottish Standard English [a] 'cat' vowel. Indeed, one can sometimes hear such speakers pronounce 'Glasgow' as [glɑzgoʊ] (showing both the back [ɑ] sound and the diphthongisation of the Scots [o]). Particularly noticeable among such speakers too is the loss of the post-vowel [r] sound in words like 'far', 'tar', 'further' and so on, a loss which is a major characteristic of Middle Class Standard English speakers.

Yet, as we have already seen, speakers can choose what they consider to be an appropriate, even prestigious, pronunciation from the usage of a social class which is lower in status than their own. A good example of this can be seen in the spread of the glottal stop among young Middle Class males (and, increasingly, females) in both Edinburgh and Glasgow, presumably the result of the perceived *caché* attached to streetwise Working Class male usage. Such changes from below – the cross-class dissemination of *vernacular* rather than *prestige* norms – are well documented, particularly so in communities where there is considerable dialect contact among speakers and especially within or in close proximity to large urban conurbations.

A good example from the South-East of England is the spread of Working Class London Cockney forms into rural east Anglia and even Norwich – for instance, *[l] vocalisation* in words like [fio] 'feel', where the [l] sound is substituted by a vowel. Here we see the effects of dialect contact between communities which are not directly contiguous, but where the prestige target exists at a geographical distance from the acquirer of the new form. This kind of phenomenon is currently active in Scotland too. A study of the fishing villages of Anstruther and Cellardyke on the Fife coast showed how Working Class pronunciation features (notably the use of the glottal stop) which are usually the preserve of urban Central Belt speakers were adopted by adolescents in these relatively isolated, non-urban, fishing communities where they had not previously been in evidence. While it is possible that these vernacular prestige forms were being adopted as one result of the presence in the fishing communities of urban incomers from the Central Belt (these speakers having a high social status as city dwellers), other, less obvious factors may also be at work.

It is a well-known feature of Working Class English in the general London area that speakers show a change in pronunciation of the dental fricatives [θ] and [ð] – the initial sounds in the words 'thick' and 'this' respectively. These speakers change these sounds into [f] and [v], so that words like 'think' and 'mother' are realised as [fɪŋk] and [mʌvɑ]. Sociolinguists have observed that these changes are beginning to appear among adolescent speakers in areas of Britain quite remote from London: e.g. in Derby and Newcastle. So it would appear that face-to-face contact between speakers of different dialects is an unlikely explanation for such events. A recent study of Glasgow speakers has also shown that this event is taking place there too (inevitably labelled **Jockney**). Although the picture is a complex one, it seems that young Working Class males and females in Glasgow are increasingly using [f] for [θ] in words like 'think', 'something', 'nothing' both in conversational, and even when they are reading word lists, in fairly formal contexts. The [v] for [ð] change, while less prominent, is also a feature of this class of speaker.

Among this group of speakers too there are very recent and observable pronunciation changes which also appear to have their origins outside Scotland. As we have already seen, for many Standard Scottish English speakers there is a clear distinction in the pronunciation of the first sound in words like 'Wales' and 'whales'. The former shows a [w] sound, as in words like 'was', 'wet', the other shows an aspirated [hw] sound [hwelz] 'whales', also in words like 'what', 'when', 'why' (all with an unaspirated [w] in Standard English). A survey of young Glasgow Working Class speakers showed the aspirated [hw] systematically being lost in words like 'whales', 'why', 'wherefore' and the like, and replaced by the unaspirated [w], as in most Standard English. Not only that but, although this change was most prominent among Working Class adolescents (particularly males again), there was evidence to suggest that it was acting as a change from below and entering the speech of young speakers (especially females) belonging to the Middle Class as well.

So, too, the stereotypically Scottish [x] sound, in words like 'loch', is being replaced by [k], so that a 'loch'/'lock' merger is appearing. A change like this has been going on for some time, as we can see in the pronunciation of the place-name Hawkhead, for what was originally Haughhead. A recent study of the speech of young people in Livingston New Town has shown a similar range of changes taking place, with the apparent exception of the [w]/[hw] opposition, which remains unaffected there, speakers keeping 'Wales' and 'whales' distinct. Data like those from Livingston seem to suggest that dialect contact with speakers from the Glasgow region is possibly leading to the introduction of Glaswegian pronunciations (and probably other linguistic features as well) throughout the Central Belt as a whole.

Innovations of the type discussed above would all seem to suggest an influence on the English language in Scotland originating from outside Scotland itself; indeed the 'fink' for 'think' and 'lock' for 'loch' as well as the 'Wales' for 'whales' innovations seem to point to an effect on the speech of young Scottish speakers from points south of the border (especially Metropolitan London). This impression is reinforced by a recent study of the ways in which *The Scottish Vowel Length Rule* (see Section 3.2(9) above) is currently realised among young speakers in Edinburgh. The researchers found that 4- to 9-year-old children in the Middle Class area of Corstorphine in Edinburgh were only partially acquiring the lengthening rule – indeed, this failure to show *The Scottish Vowel Length Rule* was particularly prevalent among those children who came from households where one or both parents were English.

It is difficult to point with certainty to any one influence for these changes that are so characteristic of young Working Class urban speech. It might seem obvious that media influence is responsible. But little research has been done in this area to prove the issue one way or the other. Indeed, the researcher in the Livingston survey found that *Eastenders* was not the preferred viewing of the adolescent group, but the American sitcom *Friends*. We might wonder, too, with the enormous popularity among older people of soaps such as *Coronation Street* and *Brookside*, why there is little or no evidence of the spread of features of North-West English dialect characteristics among speakers of Scottish (or apparently any other dialectal variety of) English.

Much recent sociolinguistic research has demonstrated that a kind of *dialect levelling* is taking place, with marked regional dialectal features being replaced by a set of British national types, some of which are not unlike Standard English forms. Such a phenomenon is perhaps most pronounced in the South and South-East of England where a kind of pan-dialectal form of the language is appearing (*Estuary English*), again especially among adolescent speakers – to the extent that it is becoming difficult to recognise major dialectal (especially pronunciation) differences in the speech of young people (particularly young Working Class females) from places as far apart as Southampton and Norwich. Perhaps the appearance of Standard and non-Standard *English* English forms in Scotland represents an extension of this process. However, it is important to bear in mind that the kinds of pronunciation changes we have been discussing above are precisely those which we would expect to occur anyway in the usual processes of phonological change; that they are occurring in different parts of the country at the same time may mean no more than that they are natural and common and have little to do with dialect contact or sociological influences. But the jury is still out in this area.

It is important to realise too that changes in pronunciation are not always in the direction of English, rather than Scottish, linguistic norms. Indeed, there is some evidence to suggest that in the eastern Border counties, pronunciation on the English side is targeted upon Scots and not, as one might intuitively expect, English (particularly urban Newcastle) prestige forms. A good example of this is in the distribution of the sound [t], [p] and [k] (the voiceless stops) when they occur in word initial position: 'Tim', 'pit', 'kit'. Typical of speakers on the English side of the border are versions of these sounds which are quite distinctly aspirated (or breathy), thus [p^h], [t^h] and [k^h]. On the other hand, speakers on the Scottish side prefer these voiceless stops to be without this following puff of air. The distinction can be visibly shown by holding a piece of paper in front of your mouth and uttering the words 'peak' and 'speak'. The former (the aspirated [p^h]) will cause the paper to visibly move, the other (the unaspirated [p]) will set off no such movement of the paper. Speakers in the Northumbrian border town of Wooler live in a sea of *aspirated* initial voiceless stops. Yet younger speakers in this market town community, when they are asked to read lists of words (i.e. when they are made conscious of their linguistic usage) produce *unaspirated* forms. In other words, they seem to perceive the Scottish pronunciation as the one having the higher prestige, despite the relative geographical proximity of a large urban conurbation in Tyneside where aspiration is the favoured realisation in formal contexts.

Yet again, younger speakers on the English side of the border show a preference for a Scottish pronunciation norm in the way they pronounce the diphthong in words like 'five', 'prize' – recall how these are the ('long') diphthongs (usually [ae] in Standard Scottish English) typical of the application of *The Scottish Vowel Length Rule* in pre voiced-fricative contexts (Section 3.2). This vowel length rule is operative too in Northumbrian English which, however, in general prefers a diphthong with a low *front* starting point – [ae] in this phonetic environment, rather than the low *back* start of the Scottish diphthong – [ae]. Younger speakers in the area around Wooler in Northumberland (especially in formal situations) seem to be changing to a diphthong with this low *back* starting point – [ae]; the difference is small, but quite audible. This latter pronunciation is absolutely typical of the usage of Scottish speakers on the *northern* side of the border. Both cases would therefore seem to suggest that dialect contact is taking place and that the target is a Scots rather than an English one. Indeed, it has even been shown that in some of the Northumbrian border towns, Middle Class women use 'refayned' diphthongal pronunciations like [ɛɪ] in words like 'five' and 'thrive' – pronunciations typical of older Middle Class women using locally prestigious speech forms in Edinburgh and Glasgow.

5.4. *Conclusions*

There is no doubt whatsoever that the English spoken in Scotland is actively undergoing change at every level – in its syntax, pronunciation and vocabulary. It needs to be stressed, however, that we as yet know relatively little about sociolinguistic variation as it affects syntax and vocabulary. The direction in which these changes are proceeding, as well as the ways in which they are being disseminated through modern society, are closely bound up with non-linguistic criteria such as age, gender and social class. Although it is very dangerous to generalise, a number of trends and tendencies seem to be emerging. (1) There is evidence to suggest that what were previously and largely Working Class forms are spreading into Middle Class usage, a process very well attested in the history of the English language in general. There is much evidence to suggest, for example, that Middle Class speakers are currently adopting characteristically Working Class forms such as the glottal stop in certain phonetic contexts. This is not to say that there is a general perception in the population that Middle Class speakers are coming to be heard as sounding more vulgar – such 'changes from below' are not always overtly observable, nor are speakers always conscious that they are occurring in their own speech. (2) The innovations taking place in the speech of modern urban Scots in particular are being led on the whole by younger speakers and young Working Class speakers at that. There seems to be a tendency for young Working Class males in the urban centres to be particularly active in the introduction of new forms of speech. (3) The traditional Middle Class urban prestige dialects such as Morningside in Edinburgh and Kelvinside in Glasgow are coming to be seen as too stereotypical even by Middle Class speakers themselves, some of whom (especially younger females) are embarrassed to be associated with the high-falutin pronunciations of their mothers. This in no way infers that Morningside and Kelvinside or other high-prestige urban dialects are disappearing – merely that they are changing. (4) Dialect levelling appears to be occurring although, as yet, there has not been sufficient research carried out to enable us to gauge its full extent or even its general direction. But it seems undeniable that (especially among adolescent Working Class speakers) there is a tendency to introduce non-Scottish (Metropolitan London) forms into their pronunciation as well as a tendency in the general Central Belt for the norms of Working Class Glaswegian to have a special influence upon this age and class group.

We must not take away the impression, however, that sociolinguistic variation and change is confined to the Central Belt. It is happening throughout the country, possibly at different rates and on different models in various regions. That we are relatively ignorant of the overall state of affairs merely reflects the lack of attention paid to issues relating to Modern Scots in general.

Suggested Reading

Chirrey, D. 1999. 'Edinburgh: Descriptive Material'. *Urban Voices.* P. Foulkes and G. Docherty. eds. London. Arnold, pp. 223–229.

Johnston, P.A. 1984. 'Variation in the Standard English of Morningside'. *English World Wide* 2, pp. 1–19.

Johnston, P.A. 1985. 'The rise and fall of the Morningside/Kelvinside dialect', in M. Görlach. ed. *Focus on Scotland.* Amsterdam. Benjamins, pp. 37--56.

Macafee, C.I. 1983. *Varieties of English Around the World: Glasgow.* Amsterdam. Benjamins.

Macaulay, R.K.S. 1978. 'Variation and consistency in Glaswegian English', in P. Trudgill. ed. *Sociolinguistic Patterns of British English.* London. Arnold, pp. 132–43.

Macaulay, R.K.S. and Trevelyan, G.D. 1977. *Language, Social Class and Education.* Edinburgh. Edinburgh University Press.

Macaulay, R.K.S. 1991. *Locating Dialect in Discourse: The Language of the Honest Men and Bonnie Lassies in Ayr.* Oxford. Oxford University Press.

Menzies, J. 1991. 'An investigation of attitudes to Scots and Glasgow dialect among secondary school pupils'. *Scottish Language* 10, pp. 30–46.

Pollner, C. 1985. 'Linguistic fieldwork in a Scottish New Town', in M. Görlach. ed. *Focus on Scotland.* Amsterdam. Benjamins, pp. 57–68.

Reid, E. 1978. 'Social and stylistic variation in the speech of children: some evidence from Edinburgh', in P. Trudgill. ed. *Sociolinguistic Patterns in British English.* London. Arnold.

Romaine, S. 1978. 'Post-vocalic [r] in Scottish English: sound change in progress?', in P. Trudgill. ed. *Sociolinguistic Patterns in British English.* London. Arnold, pp. 144–157.

Romaine, S. and E. Reid. 1976. 'Glottal sloppiness? A sociolinguistic view of urban speech in Scotland'. *Teaching English: Journal for Teachers of English in Scotland* 9, pp. 12–17.

Stuart-Smith, J. 1999. 'Glasgow: Accent and Voice Quality', in P. Foulkes and G. Docherty. eds. *Urban Voices.* London. Arnold, pp. 203–222.

Trudgill, P. 1974. 'Sociolinguistics and Scots dialects', in J.D. McClure. ed. *The Scots Language in Education. Association for Scottish Literary Studies.* Occasional Papers 3. Aberdeen.

CHAPTER SIX

Regional Variation in Modern Scots

It should be quite obvious by now that that there is no single entity which we can call Scots. We have seen, for example, how the language can vary quite markedly according to the age, social class and gender of the speaker using it, and that such variation is also a reflection of the situation in which the language is being used – that is, the level at which the speaker is conscious of using language *per se*. Yet perhaps the variation which is most immediately noticeable is that which is connected with the geographical region associated with the speaker – the speaker's **regional dialect**. There exists in modern Scotland a very wide variety of regional dialect variation, ranging from what are perceived to be the very broad types – such as rural Morayshire or Working Class Glaswegian – to the relatively close to Standard English types found in some Central Belt urban areas (Morningside/Kelvinside types). Regional differences can be very marked indeed, especially at the broad end of the scale with, for instance, the word 'who' realised as [fɑ] in the North-East (especially in the Buchan, Banff and Huntly areas) and [we] in the eastern Borders (especially Hawick), while a word like 'good' is pronounced as [gwid] in the rural hinterland of Aberdeen and as [gɪd] in Galashiels. Again, a word like 'tree' is [tri] in Aberdeen but [trɛɪ] in Hawick.

The Dialect Map suggests that there are five major dialect types: Insular (the Northern Isles), Northern (Caithness and the North-East 'shoulder'), Mid (embracing the Central Belt and Fife), Southern (the Southern Borders and Galloway area) and Ulster. These divisions correspond in part to the major geological divides in the country – the Mounth and the Southern Uplands – while patterns of settlement in the past have led to affinities between geographically dispersed areas like Angus and Caithness. The map shows too how several of the major

63

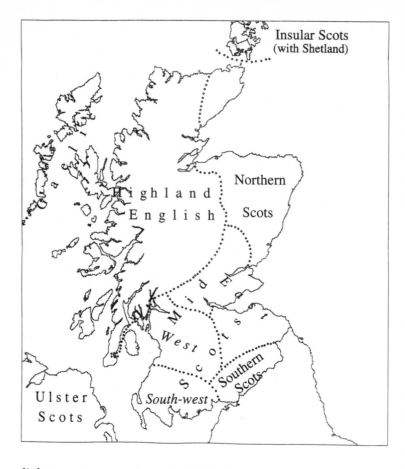

dialect regions can be sub-divided into Eastern and Western types. The large (but sparsely populated) Highland English area more or less corresponds to those parts of Scotland which in quite recent historic times were almost entirely Gaelic-speaking. Despite the usefulness of the map in providing a very general pattern of the various regional types of Scots, it is probably not very helpful to view dialect distribution in terms of precise and delimited regions, say like the North-East, the South-West, the Eastern Borders, since it is very difficult to draw precise borders where one might begin and the other end (since there are obviously areas of overlap at points of dialect contact). There is also the difficulty too of how to deal with large conurbations existing inside such broad dialect areas. For instance, is it correct to classify the form of Scots spoken in Aberdeen as the same as that spoken in the surrounding North-Eastern area, or that of the city of Edinburgh with the Scots spoken throughout the Lothian area? Are the urban centres best seen as isolated dialect islands? The problem is an extremely complex one and cannot be dealt with fully in a short survey such as this. All we can perhaps do here is to highlight some of the major characteristics of regional dialect features of Modern Scots with a very broad brush, looking in particular at some of the characteristics of regionalism at the extreme (broadest) ends of the spectrum. In particular we shall concentrate on pronunciation features, since regional variations in syntax and morphology are relatively slight and on the whole still largely uninvestigated. We shall also centre our description upon those areas of the country which seem to be the most dialectally contrastive: notably the North-East (including the Northern Isles) and the South-East Border counties.

It is absolutely vital, however, to bear in mind that regional variety is bound up inextricably with social variation. There is no regional variety which fails to show variation according to social class, gender, age and contextual factors. We have observed too how processes such as dialect contact and dialect levelling can lead to the spread of particularly urban regional types into hinterland areas. As far as we can tell at the moment, it seems to be the case that, in particular, Glasgow urban usage is spreading across the Central Belt and even into Ayrshire and the South-Western Borders. There is also much evidence to suggest that some kind of Lothianisation is occurring, whereby Edinburgh urban forms are spreading into both rural and small-town areas of the Lothians (especially Mid and East Lothian) and even as far as the eastern Border counties. We as yet know too little about the situation to assess the extent to which urban centres like Dundee and Aberdeen affect their own rural and small-town hinterland areas, but we can only assume that there is some kind of influence at work here as well.

6.1. The North-East and the Northern Isles

6.1.1. Vowel Sounds

(1) The stressed vowel in words like 'wasp', 'quarter', 'call' and 'law'. In many instances, the modern spelling of a word points to what its earlier pronunciation might have been; sound changes have taken place, but the spelling has remained fossilised. For instance, in a word like 'bought' the 'gh', which is now silent, was once pronounced (and indeed still is in some Modern Scots dialects in Aberdeenshire and the Borders). The spelling of 'wasp' and 'call' suggests that they once had a vowel like that in Modern English 'cat' or 'sat' or even the Standard English 'path' and 'after'. That [a] or [ɑ] vowel was changed (probably in the sixteenth century) to the vowel sound in words like 'got' and 'not'. In many parts of the North-East of Scotland, this change has not taken place, and speakers still use a low [ɑ] vowel in words like 'law' [lɑ], 'quarter' [kwɑrtər], 'caller' [kɑlər] and 'all' [ɑɑ]. In the same way, words like 'crofter' and 'hopper' show an [ɑ]-type vowel. (However, we should note that this is a characteristic of Scots pronunciation not confined to the North-East, since Working Class Glasgow speakers still pronounce words like 'wasp' as [wasp] and 'water' as [waʔʌr].)

(2) In much the same way, we can see from the spellings of words like 'acre', 'chamber', 'away' and 'making' that their stressed vowel would appear to have been a low [a] (like 'cat') at one time and has subsequently been changed (raised) to [e] in Standard English as well as in many Modern Scots dialects. This change did not occur in some North-Eastern dialects of Scots where pronunciations such as [mɑkər] 'maker', [ɑkər] 'acre', [əwɑɑ] 'away', [tʃɑmər] 'chamber' are regularly to be heard. This kind of pronunciation is also found in the Scots spoken in the Northern Isles, particularly in Shetland. However, what seems to occur there is that only *partial* raising of the original [a] vowel is achieved; the raising only goes as far as [ɛ], the sound in 'get', rather than all the way to [e], the sound in 'gate'. Thus we find pronunciations like [sɛl] 'sail',

and [dɛ] 'day' (with 'get' vowels), while 'take' can show no raising at all at [tak].

(3) The stressed vowel in words like 'carry', 'barracks', 'manner' and 'after' (which, as their spelling suggests, originate in [a]-type, 'cat', vowels), as well as those like 'better', 'letter' and 'pepper' (their spelling showing that they originate in [ɛ], 'get', vowels), show very distinctive pronunciations in the North-East region. All show the high front mid [e] vowel, as in 'say'. In this way we find in this dialect that words such as 'letter' and 'later', 'pepper' and 'paper' can have (close to) identical pronunciations (are **homophones**), thus [letər] for both 'later' and 'letter' and [pepər] for both 'pepper' and 'paper'. Words such as 'carry' are pronounced as [kerɪ], 'manner' as [menər] and 'barracks' as [berəks].

(4) Northern Diphthongs
A very prominent distinguishing feature of Scots (even high-prestige urban forms such as Morningside and Kelvinside) is its failure to diphthongise the vowels in words like 'say' and 'go'. Standard English has, since relatively recent historical times at any rate, changed the vowels in words like this to a diphthongal form, as in [eɪ] and [oʊ]. Scots speakers tend to maintain a monophthong in both instances, producing [se] 'say' and [go] 'go'. However, it is an equally prominent characteristic of speakers of Northern Scots in general (including North-Eastern and Northern Isles Scots, but perhaps especially a feature of the Black Isle, Moray Firth and Caithness areas) that they can diphthongise these vowels. Consequently, we find pronunciations like [tʃeɛndʒd] 'changed' and [seɛm] 'same' (with falling diphthongs – the vowel in 'say' followed by that in 'get'). Also with rising diphthongs (the vowel in 'say' followed by the vowel in 'sit') in words like 'mate', 'made', pronounced as [meɪt]/[mɛɪt], [meɪd]/[mɛɪd]. In North-Eastern dialects too we can find a rising diphthong in a word like 'seven': [sɛɪvn]. While it is probably not quite so common, the back vowels (where Standard Scots once more shows a monophthong in [o], as in 'go') can also show a diphthon-

gised form, although its occurrence is almost certainly more geographically restricted (perhaps to coastal village communities): thus words like 'stone', 'own' and 'slow' can be heard as [stoʊn], [oʊn] and [sloʊ], although it should be stressed that throughout the Northern region the [o] monophthong is probably the preferred vowel in these cases.

(5) The vowel sound in words like 'foot' and 'good'
In many regions of the country, Scots speakers regularly front the back rounded vowel in words like 'foot' and 'boot' from [u] to [ü], maintaining its lip-rounded characteristic as they do so. Among Northern and North-East Scots speakers this process of fronting can go even further, resulting in a sound which is very close to that in 'beat', so that words like 'foot' and 'feet' are almost homophonous for these speakers, who also pronounce words like 'do' as [di], 'doing' as [diən]. Likewise, a word like 'shoe' can be pronounced as [ʃi], making 'shoe' and 'she' sound identical. A fronting process as far as [ɪ] (the sound in 'bit') is quite common too among Working Class speakers in Southern Scotland, so that we get [bɪt] and [fɪt] pronunciations for 'boot' and 'foot', but for these speakers, the fronting never goes as far as [i].

6.1.2. Consonantal Sounds

(a) The Fricatives
In almost all modern Scots regional varieties (including urban types) there are groups of speakers who preserve the palatal and velar fricatives [ç] and [x] as in *nicht* ('night') and *brocht* ('brought'). The distribution of the two forms of fricative is quite predictable, the palatal fricative occurring in the vicinity of front vowels, the velar in the vicinity of back vowels – much like the *ich/ach* contrast in Modern German. The Modern English spelling suggests that these sounds were common in English in historic times, even in Southern English where they are now completely lost. Indeed, for Shakespeare or Milton these sounds would have been used in words such as 'bright' and 'daughter', grammarians contemporary with Milton

recording pronunciations like [dauxtər] and [brouxt] for 'daughter' and 'brought' (even the vowel was diphthongal at this time). Indeed, again as the spelling suggests, words such as 'laughter' and 'slaughter' also showed this [x] fricative in Southern England (indeed up until the end of the seventeenth century). Of course, they still do so for many speakers in Scotland – perhaps especially in broad versions of the North-Eastern dialects – where we can hear pronunciations such as [slaxtər] 'slaughter' and even [lɑxən] 'laughing' and [ɪnjʊx] 'enough'. In such cases, not only is the fricative present, but the subsequent change from [x] to [f] has not taken place. However, it is a very marked feature of Modern Scots in all dialectal areas (urban as well as rural) that both fricatives are being replaced by [k] (note how the famous Glasgow 'Sauchiehall Street' is now often pronounced with a [k] for the 'ch'), while recent studies of speakers in the Huntly area have shown that the fricative sound in words like 'bocht',' thocht' and 'dochter' is being entirely lost, a change led by young speakers, in particular young female speakers.

But perhaps the most distinctive consonantal feature of the North-Eastern and Northern Isles regional dialect is the treatment of the initial sound in words like 'what', 'who', 'whisky' and 'whin'. We have already seen [§3.1(7)] how Scottish Standard English differs from Standard English in showing an aspirated sound at the beginning of such words: [hwɔt], [hwɪtʃ], [hwɪskɪ] and [hwɪn], the southern dialect showing [wɔt], etc. However, speakers (not always at the broadest end of the dialectal spectrum either) will often, in the North-East of Scotland, produce a [f] sound for this word initial [hw], so that we hear [fɪt] 'what', [fɪskɪ] 'whisky', [fɪn] 'whin' and the like. At the same time, many speakers (and it probably has something to do with social class, age and gender) will use not the labio-dental [f] sound, but a bilabial fricative (like blowing out a candle) at the beginning of such words. The symbol for this bilabial fricative is [ɸ]. Thus, for a phrase like 'who's away' we can hear, especially among older speakers, a pronunciation like [ɸaɑz əwaɑ] or [faɑz əwaɑ].

The interdental fricatives [θ] and [ð] as in 'this' and 'thick' are also subject to marked variation in this dialect area. In the Aberdeenshire region, such fricatives are quite often lost at the beginnings of words, so that words like 'there', 'the' and 'that' are pronounced as [ɛr], [ə] and [at]. Such fricatives also undergo changes quite distinctive to the Northern Isles. In Shetland in particular, they tend to be replaced by the stop sounds [t] and [d]. Thus, for example, a word such as 'three' can be pronounced as [tri], while 'this', 'that' and 'they' are heard as [dɪs], [dat] and [de], even 'nothing' appearing as [nɔdn], while [fadəm] for 'fathom' can also be heard.

(b) Other consonantal features

We have seen earlier [§3.2(5)] how Scottish Standard English is, much like General American, a dialect in which the [r] sound is pronounced after vowels. Thus, we have [kar] 'car', [far] 'far' and the like, as against Standard English where the [r] has been lost in the last one hundred and fifty years or so, as in [faɑ] and [kaɑ]. In the North-East of Scotland, however, this [r] sound on occasion has a special shape, speakers producing what is known as the *uvular r* (symbol [ʀ]) where the tongue is retracted far back on to the roof of the mouth and some friction generated. In this way we find pronunciations like [biʀət] 'buried' and [tʃʌʀtʃ] 'church'. Such an [ʀ] sound is common too in the North-East of England (it is a marked feature of older Geordie speakers – the 'Northumbrian burr') and is not altogether unlike the pharyngeal (strangulated) [r] sound ([ʕ]) we have already described as a feature of Working Class young adults in both Glasgow and Edinburgh [§5:pp. 53–54].

Another, and possibly declining, characteristic of this dialect is the way in which speakers insert the [j] sound (the first sound in a word like 'you') before the stressed vowel in words like 'book' and 'hook', producing pronunciations such as [bjʊk] and [hjʊk]. After this fashion too we find words like enough as [ɪnjʊx] 'enough', [njatər] 'natter', [kjɔrn] 'corn' as well as [hjɔwən] 'hoeing'.

Consider too a word like 'media'. For some speakers this word has three syllables [midia]. For others it has only two: [midja]. It is interesting to notice how the presence of a [j]-

sound in a word like this, as well as in words like 'nature', 'culture', can have the effect of turning the preceding consonant into a fricative-like sound (the first and final sound in word like 'church' or 'judge'), thus [midja]/[midʒə] 'media', and [kʌltjər]/[kʌltʃər] 'culture'. It is a prominent feature of North-Eastern Scots that this [j] adding, and subsequent change of [t] to [tʃ] does not take place, and speakers produce forms like [netər] 'nature', [pɪktər] 'picture' and [kʌltər] 'culture'.

Although it is in all likelihood a recessive characteristic of the North-Eastern and Northern Isles dialects, and probably only to be heard with any frequency at the broad end of the dialect scale (and then possibly restricted to older speakers), there is some evidence to show that speakers will produce both initial consonants in words such as 'know', 'knee', 'gnat' and 'gnome'. Thus [kno] 'know', [kni] 'knee', and [gnɑt] 'gnat', and even [knʌif] for 'knife'. As the spelling suggests, such pronunciations were historically the norm with such words (indeed there is evidence to show that they were still used among speakers in the South-East of England as late as the nineteenth century). Another apparently declining feature of this region's dialect is the change of [tʃ] to [ʃ], making words like 'chip' and 'ship' homophonous.

6.2. The Southern Dialects

The geographical area covered by the Southern dialects, extending from the Western Border in Dumfries and Galloway to the Eastern Border in Berwickshire, is very large. It is certainly the case that we are not dealing with a unified dialect across the whole area, and there are marked differences in pronunciation between speakers in, say, Hawick and those in Newton Stewart. However, it is certainly true that speakers across the area still have a strong sense that they speak a distinctive dialect, despite the fact that there has been a noticeable spread of Central Belt forms – especially from Glasgow and Edinburgh – into the entire Borders region in recent years. There is even a strong local feeling that certain communities have distinctive dialects, with a powerful dialect allegiance to speech habits in places such as Hawick, Jedburgh and Kelso. There is also a two-way flow of influence across the English border (perhaps particularly marked in the Western Border Counties), although, as we have already seen, the influence works both ways, there being evidence to suggest that speakers in rural Northumbria target Scots forms in formal contexts rather than those characteristic of the Tyneside conurbation (§5.3: pp. 59–60).

6.2.1. *Southern Diphthongs*

We have already seen immediately above that in words like 'mate' and 'pay' Scots in general tends to show a monophthongal vowel in [e], while Northern dialects produce a diphthong. This diphthongal pronunciation is characteristic of the Southern dialects as well. In several areas of the Borders, words like 'state', 'mate' show falling diphthongs like [iɪ] (the vowel in 'see' followed by the vowel in 'sit') and [iɛ] (the vowel in 'see' followed by the vowel in 'get') – not unlike Northumbrian usage. Even words like 'pay' and 'say' – with [e] in Scottish Standard English – are diphthongised to a form which is almost homophonous with the diphthong in a word like 'bite'. Thus we hear pronunciations like [pʌɪ] for 'pay'. Although it is again probably restricted to older and broader speakers, we can also still hear diphthongal pronunciations for a word like 'goat' or 'coat' where the Scots [o] vowel has been raised to [u] and diphthongised, so that we get [gʊət] 'goat' and [kʊət] 'coat' pronunciations, once again not at all unlike the usage found among older, working-class speakers in Northumbria and County Durham (even in urban contexts like Newcastle and Durham City).

In the Border region too there is a tendency for speakers to realise the vowel in a word like 'tree' as a diphthong [trɛɪ] (the 'get' vowel followed by the 'sit' vowel). Indeed, such a pronunciation is certainly perceived locally as a hallmark, or stereotype, of Hawick dialect speech. But diphthongal pronunciations in words of this type, such as 'meet', 'feet', 'see' (all with [i] in most Scots) are still relatively common both on the Eastern and Western sides of the Border and, indeed, in Cumbria and Northumberland as well (although the form of the diphthong there is often [eɪ] rather than [ɛɪ]). Yet there is recent evidence to suggest that diphthongal pronunciations like this are on the decline, reserved for older broader speakers, and becoming less common among younger speakers who are adopting the more general Scots and Standard English [i] form in 'tree' words.

The spelling of words like 'grow' and 'know' suggests that at one time in their history their vowels were, in fact, diphthongal – a fact supported by much historical evidence. In non-Working Class forms of Modern Scots as a whole, these original diphthongs have become simple vowel sounds, thus [gro] 'grow' and [no] 'know'. It is a marked characteristic of Working Class Border Scots, in particular when the speaker is using language in an unselfconscious context, for these original diphthongs to be realised – often as [ʌʊ] or [au] – so that the vowel space in 'grow' resembles that in 'growl' (the 'cat' vowel followed by the 'book' vowel).

But perhaps one of the most characteristic features of the vowel system of the Southern Border counties lies in the way speakers there pronounce the vowels in words like 'dot' and 'dote'. In common with many Working Class speakers in the urban areas of the Central Belt, Border Scots speakers will merge the vowels in words of this type under the (higher) [o] vowel; thus 'cot' is pronounced like 'coat'. However, and particularly in Berwickshire and in the Peebles area, this [o] vowel is centralised or fronted to [ø]. A way to hear an approximation to this sound is to produce the vowel in words like 'say' or 'they' but with a deliberate and exaggerated rounding of the lips. This development occurs too in some North-East dialects.

Finally, it is a marked characteristic of the vowel system in Border Scots that the vowel in words like 'cat', 'sat' and 'mat' is backed, and pronounced not unlike the sound [ɑ] in Standard Southern British English 'bath' and 'path' words. However, probably only among older speakers, the vowel in such words is pronounced like the [ɔ] vowel in 'caught', so that there can be a 'cat'/'caught' merger for some speakers, both words sounding like 'cot'.

6.2.2. *Consonantal Sounds*

Very marked consonantal dialect features are almost all now characteristic of older and usually Working Class speakers in the region although, as we might expect, they are more common in the rural hinterland than in towns like Hawick, Jedburgh or Newton Stewart. Up until a hundred years ago speakers in the Eastern Border counties were recorded as pronouncing the initial [w] in words like 'write', 'wrong' and 'wrestle' (with some North-Eastern dialect speakers showing [vrɪçt] for 'wright'). But there seems to be little evidence of this phenomenon today. Likewise, it appears that the substitution of a stop [d] sound for a fricative [ð] in initial position in words like 'they' and 'them' (a feature we have also seen in North-Eastern dialects – §6.1.2) is also still occasionally to be heard (perhaps most commonly in the South-Western Border area – mainly Wigtonshire), but this too is dying out among younger speakers. In the Eastern border, especially in places like Kirk Yetholm close to the English border, we can still hear older Working Class speakers produce the characteristic Northumbrian or Durham 'burr' – the uvular [ʀ] – but the further from the English border the speaker lives, the less likelihood is there that this sound will appear. Even in places like Kirk Yetholm and Roxburghshire, this type of [ʀ] sound is hardly ever used by the younger generation (among whom it is dying out even in Northumberland).

In many parts of the Borders we can hear a contrast (also a feature of some Working Class Glasgow speakers) whereby words beginning with [θr], words such as 'three' and 'through', are pronounced with initial [fr]. Thus 'three' and 'free' are homophonous for these speakers. Another change involving fricative consonants is the alternation (perhaps mainly in the Eastern border counties) between [tʃ] and [ʃ], so that 'chip' and 'ship', 'chop' and 'shop' can sound the same – recall too the Border place-name Shillingham, now Chillingham. In another contrast not too unlike this, probably also confined to place-names in the eastern side of the Borders, we see what originally was a [g] sound in names like Birgham and Bellingham changed to a fricative [dʒ], thus: [bɪrdʒəm] and [bɛlɪndʒəm].

6.3. *Urban Dialects of the Central Belt*

6.3.1. *Glasgow*

(a) **Vowel Sounds**

One of the most obvious and salient features of Working Class Glasgow speech (although there is evidence that the pheno-menon is spreading into Middle Class usage as well) is the tendency to lower and centralise the vowel in words like 'sit' and 'hill'. For many speakers, for instance, the words 'hill' and 'hull' are almost homophonous. The 'hill' vowel, in fact, is a centralised low mid [ɛ̈], and its widespread use for the higher and fronter [ɪ] sound leads to much near-homophony in this dialect, with 'pit'/'putt', 'lick'/'luck' and 'kill'/'cull' mergers taking place. An effect of this lowering can be seen too in words like 'foot'. In common with many regional dialects of Scots, speakers in Glasgow will front the [u] vowel as far as [ɪ], thus making 'fit' and 'foot' sound alike. As a result of the lowering and centring of the [ɪ] sound, a word like 'boot' comes to be pronounced close to 'but'. This phenomenon also lies behind the near similarity in the pronunciation of 'bull' and 'Bill' among many Glasgow speakers. But, perhaps above all other pronunciation phenomena in Modern Scots, it is the geographical spread of this [ɛ̈] for [ɪ] pronunciation which is most marked, the lowered/centralised form appearing in many parts of the country, often remote (e.g. in Dumfries and Galloway) from the Central Belt itself.

As we have already noted, the spelling of words such as 'wash', 'want', 'wasp' and 'water' suggests that at one time in their history their stressed vowel must have been like that found today in words like 'cat' and 'sat'. Indeed, the change of the [a] vowel in such words to the vowel in 'got' only dates in Standard English from the late eighteenth and early nine-teenth centuries. For many speakers of English in Glasgow, this change has not occurred and an [a] vowel as in 'cat' is still used in such words (showing an initial [w] sound) – recall Rab C. Nesbit's *swally* 'swallow').

In words such as 'home', 'most', 'alone' and 'floor' Glasgow speakers, in common with those from several other geographical areas, will front the [o] sound to [e], 'floor' and 'flair' sounding the same. This usage is, of course, mainly confined to Working Class speakers and stigmatised elsewhere. Indeed, it may be confined to quite a restricted set of words, even for Working Class speakers: words like 'both', 'whole', 'hole', 'nobody' and 'no' in phrases like 'I'll no do it'.

The high-mid front vowel [e] (as in 'say') – particularly when it occurs before an [r] sound – can for many Glasgow speakers be lowered to the sound of the vowel in 'get' – [ɛ]. Words like 'chair', 'hair', 'stair' and 'there', and even the non-standard pronunciations of 'floor' and 'more' with [e], are found in Glasgow with the 'get' vowel. Interestingly, there are many Glaswegians who will assert that this [e]/[ɛ] contrast is a signal of religious affiliation, Protestants using the [fler] pronunciation, Catholics the [flɛr]. However, despite the strong sense many speakers have that this is a real phenomenon, sociolinguistic study has yet to find convincing evidence that it is actually a genuine feature of local usage.

There are, of course, a whole range of other characteristics of Glasgow regional speech which are too numerous to mention in a short survey like this, but one should perhaps not leave the subject without mentioning the tendency (especially among older speakers) to use a diphthong like the one in 'tile' ([ʌɪ], the 'but' vowel followed by the 'sit' vowel), in words like 'boil', 'join'. Such speakers can also use a diphthong like this in words such as 'way', 'stay' and even 'day'. Finally, perhaps, we might mention local treatments of the [a] 'cat' vowel: firstly, [a] is raised to the 'get' vowel in words like 'carry' as in a 'carry-oot': [kɛrɪ ʊt], secondly, this vowel can appear as [ɔ] (especially before [n] or [r]) so that we find that for many Glaswegians a 'tramcar' is (or was) a [kɔr], waiting for which could, on occasion, involve a lot of [stɔnɪn] 'standing'.

(b) Consonantal Sounds

We have already seen some of the more recent characteristics of the pronunciation of Scots in the Glasgow area in our discussion of sociolinguistic distribution and change in Section 5.3. We should bear in mind that there seems to be some evidence for a spread of some Central Belt forms (notably those originating from Glasgow) into other areas of Scotland (particularly the Border counties). Likewise, there seems to be evidence that there is a levelling taking place between Glasgow and Edinburgh pronunciations, several features of which are now common to both urban communities. Perhaps most obvious among these is the widespread use of glottal stops for [p], [t] and [k] in several environments, notably between vowels ([paʔʌr] 'patter', [sʌʔʌr] 'supper', [fʌʔɪn] 'fucking') and at the ends of words ([hɪʔ ɪʔ] 'hit it'). Glasgow speakers are particularly inclined to substitute a vowel sound (usually [u] or [o]) for [l] at the ends of words, such that 'tool' is pronounced as [tuo] and 'meal' as [mio] – *[l]-vocalisation* (p. 56).

Other features of the Glasgow consonantal system (perhaps mostly confined to Working Class speakers in informal contexts) are (a) the use of the tap [r] for [t] when it occurs between vowels (a context for the glottal stop as well), so that we find [bʌrʌr] 'butter'. At the same time, this tap [r] can substitute in this same context for the fricative [θ], thus [bɔrʌr] for 'bother' and [brʌrʌr] 'brother'. (b) [h] can often appear for [θ], so that we get [sʌmhɪn] for 'something', while the [θ] itself may be completely lost, as in 'Rothesay' [rɔse] and even [klez] 'clothes'. (c) Some words beginning with [θ] are pronounced with a sound close to (but not quite identical with) the first in a word like 'she', thus [θri] 'three' can sound like 'shree'. (d) In words where the consonants [r], [m], and [n] appear together at the end of syllables, the speaker will often insert a vowel between groups or clusters like [rm] and [rn] – thus we get [gɪrʌlz] 'girls' , [farʌm] 'farm' and [fɔrʌm] 'form'.

(c) Intonation

There is a very distinctive rise and fall of the voice (its pitch) in the speech of many Glasgow speakers. In particular, there is a strong tendency for the pitch of the voice to rise at the end of sentences, even when these sentences are not question sentences. For example, while we would expect the pitch of the voice to rise at the end of an interrogative sentence like: 'Are you going home now?', it is common to find such a pitch rise also appearing in a statement sentence like 'I like the Celtic'. This is a phenomenon also common in the speech of young Australian women, and (naïve) observers have suggested it represents an inherent insecurity and uncertainty in the psyche of the speaker. Such claims can be safely ignored.

6.3.2. Edinburgh

(a) Vowel Sounds

The vowel sounds of Edinburgh speakers do not differ significantly from those of Glasgow. However, there are a few contrasts worth noting. While some Glasgow speakers will make vowels long in contexts which *The Scottish Vowel Length Rule* (Section 3.1) would not predict (e.g. 'a big cat' [ə bɪg kaaʔ]), Edinburgh speakers are much less inclined to do this. At the same time, it is worth noting that, for many (especially Working Class speakers) the 'cat' vowel in Edinburgh is further back, i.e. it is more like [ɑ] (as in Standard English 'path'); in Glasgow, the sound is generally like [a]. It is likely too that the final vowel in words like 'barrow' or 'window' is [e] for Edinburgh speakers, rather than the [a] or [o] of Glasgow. This final [e] sound is also characteristic of words like 'lovely', 'nicely' in Edinburgh, where Glasgow shows [ɪ].

(b) Consonantal Sounds

The consonantal characteristics of Edinburgh speech are very like those of Glasgow, showing significant glottalisation as well as the substitution of [h] for [θ] in words like 'nothing' and 'something'. However, there does seem to be some evidence that [l] vocalisation is not such a persistent feature (especially among older speakers). Edinburgh Middle Class female speakers (as we have already seen: Section 5.2) appear to have a local and characteristic voiced alveolar approximant [ɹ] sound syllable finally in words like 'car' and 'far', although even this pronunciation may now be appearing among the same high-prestige social group in Glasgow.

6.3.3. Ulster Scots

While there was much contact between and immigration from Gaelic-speaking Scotland into what is now Ulster from as early as the twelfth century, the major influx of Lowland Scots-speaking people, particularly into what is now County Antrim, only dates from the late sixteenth century. At that time the North-East part of County Antrim in particular was populated quite densely with Lowland Scots-speaking migrants. There appears to have been a much smaller impact of this kind of migration into North-West Ulster and in (London)Derry. However, it is important to stress that the migration was a two-way process, both from South-West Scotland into Ulster and from Ulster into Scotland. There was, at the same time, some English immigration into Northern Ireland in the sixteenth and seventeenth centuries, and Scots and English language speakers existed side by side. However, the population ratio was very much biased in favour of the Scots-speaking community in the early settlement period.

6.3.3.1. Some Ulster Scots pronunciation characteristics

The Scots spoken in Ulster is quite distinctive from that in Scotland itself, although both dialects have common characteristics. We need to be aware of the fact too that Ulster Scots, like its mainland variety, varies according to sociolinguistic factors such as class, age and gender, rural versus urban. The following represent a few of the defining characteristics of the pronunciation of modern Ulster Scots:

(a) Mainland Scots speakers typically show a high mid vowel monophthong in words such as 'safe' [sef] and 'way' [we], even though, as their spelling suggests, the vowels in such words have a separate historical source, the former a monophthong, the latter a diphthong. In Ulster Scots, this separate source feature is recognised through different pronunciations for 'say' and 'safe' words. For the former, Ulster Scots uses a characteristically lowered [ɛɛ] vowel, thus [wɛɛ] 'way' and [dɛɛ] 'day', while for words like 'same' and 'save' we hear falling diphthongs in [eə], thus [seəm] and [seəv]. It is interesting to note too how this monophthong/diphthong contrast is also a reflection of the presence or absence of morphology (word endings to show past tense or plural number, for instance), thus: [deəz] 'daze', but [dɛɛz] 'days' (with plural morphology) and [breəd] 'the donkey brayed' versus [brɛɛd] 'braid cloth'.

(b) Not unlike some prestigious Edinburgh older female use, we find Working Class speakers in cities such as Belfast pronouncing words like 'beg' and 'bag', 'pack' and 'peck' as homophones, with an [ɛ] vowel. Indeed, for some speakers there can be a kind of [a]/[ɛ] interchange, seen in the often quoted pronunciation of 'jet lag' as [dʒaʔ lɛg] and [takstʌɪl fɛktərɪ] for 'textile factory'!

(c) A characteristic of Working Class Belfast speech is the tendency to diphthongise short vowels (especially before voiced stop consonants) as in [bɛəd] 'bed', [lɛəg] 'leg' and [hɛəd] head.

(d) Very distinctive of many modern Ulster Scots speakers too is the use, in words like 'mouth', 'town' and 'now' (where a diphthong like [au] would be used in Standard English), of a diphthongal form not unlike that found in Standard English words like 'price', 'nice' and 'dice'. Thus, for 'mouth', we hear from some Ulster Scots speakers a form like [məɪθ], and [səɪθ] for 'south'.

(e) As with some varieties of mainland Scots, Working Class Belfast Ulster Scots can show a merger between [a] 'cat' and [ɔ] 'got' sounds , such that words like 'man', 'grass' and 'bad' are often to be heard with the vowel sound of words like 'got' and 'not'. Recall here mainland Working Class urban Scots pronunciations of words like 'candle' and 'handle' as [kɔnəl] and [hɔnəl], typical too of areas of Belfast.

(f) Although the phenomenon is probably on the wane, and reserved for older (male) speakers in Belfast Working Class areas, we can still find a tendency to insert a front palatal glide [j] after initial palatal consonants like [k], so that a word like 'cab' can be pronounced as [kjɑɑb]/[kjɛɛb] and 'cart' as [kjɛɛrt] (the double vowel symbol signifying that the vowel is long). Such pronunciations are well recorded in London speech in the late eighteenth century, as well as in some varieties of Modern English still spoken in the Caribbean.

6.3.4. Highland English

Our dialect map shows that there is a large geographical area of Scotland (albeit sparsely populated) where a distinctive regional dialect is spoken – Highland English – although it can show variation from place to place in the region. A great part of this region was almost entirely Gaelic-speaking up until the late eighteenth century, although from that time the rise of English and the demise of Gaelic was quite swift. It would appear that once an English-speaking political and economic elite was established in the Highlands and Islands, the use of the English language increasingly became the norm. Indeed there were attempts to suppress the use of Gaelic in schools and in the church throughout the eighteenth and nineteenth centuries. One result of this was that Gaelic was often confined to particular discourse contexts – speakers using English when discussing matters relating to trade and commerce, Gaelic in other contexts (day-to-day topicality and with reference to matters ecclesiastical). The differing roles of English and Gaelic are still to be observed in communities like those in Harris and other parts of the Hebrides, but even here younger speakers are choosing English increasingly as the prestige language. Overall there has been a massive intrusion of English into the historic Gaelic-speaking areas of Scotland, to such an extent that there appear to be no speakers alive today whose sole language is Gaelic, although revivals of Gaelic as a second language are having some success.

Highland English has been described as 'Standard English on a Gaelic substratum' (Mather and Speitel:1986:8b). That is, the form of English targeted by Gaelic speakers was not Scots, but Standard English – indeed, Highland English has traditionally shown little influence of Lowland Scots at any level, even vocabulary, but this situation may be changing and Scots may now be having more of an influence than in the past. Highland English has gone unstudied for a long time and our knowledge of its characteristics is probably the most scanty of all the Scots dialect areas. As one might expect, there may well be cross-language influence, with Highland English showing features of Gaelic and vice versa. For instance, it seems that a Highland English syntactic construction like 'I was reading Shakespeare all my life' reflects the fact that Gaelic has no syntactic mechanism for showing an activity that is continuously engaged in in the past, as in the English construction: 'I have read (have been reading) Wordsworth every day since I was at school'. Again, the Gaelic conjunction *agus* 'and' is able to introduce clauses which modify the main clause in different ways from the English conjunction *and*. Thus, we find in Highland English constructions like: 'You should not be drinking whisky and you taking those pills', where the *and* denotes a relationship something like 'since' as in 'while/since you are taking those pills, you should not be drinking whisky', a function *agus* is apparently capable of in Gaelic. However, the precise status of syntactic constructions like 'He has arms good for the weight lifting', sometimes found in literary materials and parodies of Highland speech, is perhaps apocryphal at best.

On pronunciation grounds we are perhaps on firmer soil. Highland English speakers often appear to use voiceless forms of sounds rather than voiced (the vocal cords remaining unactivated in the voiceless context). For instance we can hear pronunciations of words like 'butter' with an intial [p] rather than [b]; 'glad' with initial [k] rather than [g] and 'bleed' with final [t] rather than [d]. This voicing difference extends to the [f]/[v] contrast as well, Highland English speakers often making 'ferry' and 'very' sound homophonous. In fact, Gaelic has no voiced fricatives like [z] as in 'girls', [ʒ] in 'treasure' or [dʒ] in 'judge', so Highland English speakers tend to produce voiceless forms, realising: [gʌrls], [trɛsjər] and [tʃʌtʃ]. Likewise, Gaelic lacks the interdental fricatives [θ] as in 'thin' and [ð] as in 'the', and will tend to substitute the former, especially, with [s], so that 'thin' is pronounced as [sɪn] and 'mouth' and 'mouse' are homophones. Gaelic has a rule in its sound structure whereby sequences of [r] and [s] come to be pronounced as a single sound, not unlike the initial sound – [ʃ] – in words like 'shoe' and 'shine'. As a result of this many Highland English speakers (perhaps especially those from the Hebridean areas) will pronounce words like 'farce' and 'parcel' as though they were pronounced something like [faʃ] and [paʃəl]. Finally, many Highland English speakers have only one kind of [l] sound in their sound system and that is the back or 'dark' [ł], a sound restricted in many varieties of English to positions following back vowels, as in words like 'gull' and 'sullen'. For many Highland English speakers this sound appears everywhere, even in words like 'hill', 'silly', 'Milly', where in Standard English the front or 'clear' [l] would be found.

Suggested Reading

Barry, M. and Tilling, P.M. 1986. eds. *The English Dialects of Ulster.* Hollywood, Down. The Ulster Folk and Transport Museum.

Catford, J.C. 1958. 'Vowel Systems of Scots Dialects'. *Transactions of the Philological Society*, pp. 10–17.

Dieth, E. 1932. *A Grammar of the Buchan Dialect.* Cambridge. Heffer.

Glauser, B. 1974. *The Scottish-English Linguistic Border.* Bern. Francke.

Harris, J. 1984. 'English in the North of Ireland', in P. Trudgill. ed. *Language in the British Isles.* Cambridge. Cambridge University Press.

Harris, J. 1985. *Phonological Variation and Change.* London. Cambridge University Press, pp. 10–63 for Ulster Scots

Harris, J. 1993. 'The Grammar of Irish English', in J. and L. Milroy. eds. *Real English.* London. Longman, pp. 137–184.

Hettinga, J. 1981. 'Standard and dialect in Anstruther and Cellardyke'. *Scottish Literary Journal. Supplement* 14, pp. 37–48.

Hughes, A. and Trudgill, P. 1979. *English Accents and Dialects.* London. Arnold.

*Johnston, Paul. 1983. 'Irregular Style Patterns in Edinburgh Speech'. *Scottish Language* 2, pp. 1–19.

*Johnston, Paul. 1997. 'Regional Variation', in C. Jones. ed. *The Edinburgh History of the Scots Language.* Edinburgh University Press. Edinburgh.

Lodge, K.R. 1984. *Studies in the Phonology of Colloquial English.* London. Chapter 4.

Macafee, C.I. 1983. *Glasgow: Varieties of English Around the World.* Amsterdam. Benjamins.

Macafee, C.I. 1998. 'Dialect erosion with special reference to urban Scots', in A. Fenton and MacDonald, D.A. eds. *Studies in Scots and Gaelic.* Edinburgh. Canongate Academic, pp. 69–80.

McArthur, T. 1992. ed. *Oxford Companion to the English Language.* Oxford. Oxford University Press: entries under *Dialect in Scotland; Edinburgh; Glasgow; Gutter Scots; Morningside and Kelvinside Accents; Orkney and Shetland Dialects; Scottish English; The Scottish Vowel Length Rule.*

*Mather, J.Y. and Speitel, H.H. 1986. eds. *The Linguistic Atlas of Scotland.* Scots Section. Volume III. London. Croom Helm.

Murray, J.A.H. 1873. *The Dialect of the Southern Counties of Scotland,* London. Asher.

Wettstein, P. 1942. *The Phonology of a Berwickshire Dialect.* Zürich. Schuler.

Zai, R. 1942. *The Phonology of the Morebattle Dialect.* Lucerne. Raeber.

CHAPTER SEVEN

The Representation of Scots in Literary Texts

Attempts at the representation of Scots speech in literary materials are, of course, of very long standing. We have only to look at the novels of Walter Scott – in particular, perhaps, the speech of the Scots characters in *The Heart of Midlothian* – and those of Smollett to see the length of the pedigree of this tradition. The practice continues apace today, of course, both in the novels of writers like Kelman and Gray, but also in comic-strip formats such as *The Broons* and *Oor Wullie* as well as in the poetry of the modern Scots literary renaissance. It is to be seen too in parodies of Modern Scots of the type which were in Stanley Baxter's *Parliamo Glasgo* broadcasts in the 1960s and 1970s. In these were used representations such as: *Era/Erza* 'there is', as in *Erzaperapersonrafler* 'there is a pair of pears on the floor'; *zatso* 'Is that so?' and *snofer* 'It's not fair' and the like. But the problems faced by any author wishing to represent non-standard language in a written form are formidable. A fully detailed representation of the actual sounds made by non-standard speakers (achieved, say, by using a phonetic alphabet) would be far too difficult for the reader to take on board (and probably too expensive for the publisher to produce). The dilemma is well described by the Glasgow writer Tom Leonard (1984:73; Macauley 1992:281):

> Yi write doon a wurd, nyi sayti yirsell, that's no thi way a say it. Nif yi tryti write it doon thi way yi say it, yi end up wi thi page covered in letters stuck thigither, nwee dots above hof thi letters, in fact yi end up wi wanna they thingz yi needti huv took a course in phonetics ti be able ti read.

The author has to strike a balance between interpretability (i.e. relative closeness to the standard orthographic system) and a means of signalling that non-standard (and perhaps dialect-specific) language is being represented. If the density of the former is too great, then there can be severe problems of communication and interpretation; too small and the regional, non-standard effect is diluted. Even the apparently dialectally dense Leonard piece can illustrate this dilemma. Notice, for example, how there are many words still spelt with the standard orthography, even though they would have quite distinct (in this instance Glaswegian) pronunciations: 'write'; 'that's'; 'way'; 'page'; 'letters'; 'covered'; 'phonetic' and many others. Most noticeably, items like 'letters' and 'that's' would almost certainly be pronounced in this context with glottal stops where the author uses a 't' symbol. Perhaps the glottal is not shown because there is nothing in the standard alphabet set which can obviously be used for it, though one might suggest that (as some authors have done) an apostrophe could have been used as a signal, thus: 'wri'e'; 'phone'ics' and so on. But we need to notice too that Leonard's non-standard spelling is used not just to show Glaswegian or even Scots-specific phenomena. Spellings like *nyi* 'and you' and *needti* 'need to' serve to illustrate *continuous* or *fast speech* characteristics which are a feature of most (even Standard) English spontaneous speech usage. Indeed, the author even misses some obvious instances of these in his text. It is unlikely that in spontaneous conversation a speaker would say 'in fact you': more likely would be something that could be represented by *in facyi* and so on. Notice too how a spelling like *thingz* merely reflects the general English voicing assimilation of the plural morpheme 's' to the voiced value of the preceding sound, and has no particular Scots connotations. The non-standard spelling, in cases like this, reflects the *standard* pronunciation, not any dialectally specific one.

Perhaps we can best illustrate some of these issues by considering the non-standard spelling system used to illustrate Modern Scots vernacular taken from Alison Kermack's *The Wee Tatty*:

He goat the idea offy the telly. Heard oan the news this Chinese boy hud ritten 2000 characters oan a singul grainy rice. Well o coarse, he kidny rite Chinese an he dooted if thur wiz any rice in the hoose (unless mebby in the chinky cartons fo last nite). Butty liked the idea. Whit wi the asbestos fi wurk damajin his lungs an him oan the invalidity an that. Well, he hudda loatty time tay himsel an no much munny ti day anyhin wi it. Anny didny reckon he hud long tay go noo. It wid be nice, yi ken, jist tay leeve sumhin behind that peepul wid mebby notice. Jist a wee thing.

So wunce the bairnz wur offty skule an the wife wiz offty wurk, he cleared the kitchin table an hud a luke in the cubburds. Rite enuff, nay rice. He foond sum tattys but. Thottyd better scrub thum furst. So he did. Then he took thum back tay the table. He picked the smollist wun soze it wizny like he wiz cheatin too much, anny began tay rite aon it wi a byro. He stied ther aw day. Kept on gawn, rackiniz brains an straynin tay keepiz hand fi shakin. Efter 7 oors o solid con-sen-tray-shun, he ran ooty space. Heed manijd tay rite 258 swayr wurds oan the wee tatty. He sat back tae huv a luke. Even tho heed scrubd it, it wiz still a bit durty-lukin an it wuz that fully ize yi kidny see the ritin very well. Bit still. He felt heed acheeved sumhin.

Non-standard spellings are rather dense in this text and comprise nearly half of all the words used. They fall into three distinct types: (1) where they reflect regional and social class Modern Scots usage, (2) where they represent the characteristics of rapid, continuous speech (without any necessary connection with Scots usage), and (3) where they are merely non-standard and have no special Scots significance.

In the first group, it is mainly **vowel sounds** that the author tends to signal as most saliently Scots:

(a) The Scots 'goat'/'got' merger. As we have seen earlier, it is a salient characteristic of Working Class (especially Central Belt) usage to use the vowel in a word like 'goat' ([o]) in words where the standard language uses the vowel in 'got' ([ɔ]) and vice versa. Many writers use the convention of spelling the [o] vowel as 'oa' and the [ɔ] vowel as 'au' or 'aw'. In our text we find: *loatty* 'lot of'; *oan* 'on'; *goat* 'got'; *gawn* 'going'.

(b) The vowel in a word like 'house' in much non-standard Scots usage is generally non-diphthongal, instead of an [au] diphthong, the (original historical) [u] vowel is used. Thus, we find: *ooty* 'out of'; *oors* 'ours'; *dooted* 'doubted'; *foond* 'found'.

(c) Perhaps the most commonly utilised signal of Scots in the text is that which shows vowels being lowered before [r]. That is, cases where words such as 'work', 'first' have a distinctive [ʌ] sound, as in the vowel in 'bus' and 'must', and have the [r] sound fully pronounced. This in contrast to standard British English where not only is the [r] sound lost, but the vowel has a sound quite like that in the first syllable of words like 'about' and 'alone'. Instances in the text include: *cubburds* 'cupboards', *wur* 'were', *wurk* 'work', *wurds* 'words' and several others.

(d) Although perhaps confined to a small set of words, non-Standard Scots will make the [u] vowel in words like 'do' and 'to' sound like that in 'say' and 'may' – the [u] vowel is fronted and lowered to [e]. In the text we find the customary symbol combination 'ae' used for this phenomenon: *tae* 'to', *dae* 'do'.

(e) Another fronting phenomenon in Modern Scots (probably Standard as well as non-Standard) involves the vowel sound in words like 'book' and 'look'. This vowel is pronounced quite far forward in the mouth, with much lip-rounding, and is not unlike the sound of the vowel in a word like 'see' pronounced with the lips rounded. The symbol for this sound is [ü]. Kermack does not use a specialised vowel symbol for this sound, preferring to spell the words in question with a final <e>, thus *skule* 'school' and *luke* 'look'.

(f) Although this phenomenon too may be restricted to a relatively small set of individual words, many Central Belt Working Class speakers pronounce the vowel in words like 'stay', 'pay' and 'way' as though they were diphthongs. The diphthong used is [ʌɪ] (the 'bus' plus the 'sit' vowel), not unlike the way these speakers pronounce the vowel space in words like 'boil' and 'joiner'. Kermack uses an 'i' graph to represent this diphthong, since that graph (as in words like 'night' and 'right') often represents a diphthong, and a diphthong which is not unlike the one in 'boil' and 'toil' and this particular pronunciation of 'stay': *stied* 'stayed'.

(g) Kermack spells the word 'people' as *peepul* in her text. It is not altogether clear what this signifies other than that the speaker is meant to be producing a vowel which is long: [piipʌl]. Although we would not expect a long vowel in this context – bearing in mind the way that *The Scottish Vowel Length Rule* tends to make vowels long in *pre-voiced* contexts only – scholars have noticed that it is a feature of current Central Belt urban Scots (especially among Working Class speakers) to lengthen *all* vowels when they are taking the main stress in the word. Such a phenomenon has come to be known as the Glasgow *drawl*. The double <ee> spellings in *heed* 'head' and *acheeved* 'achieved' may likewise represent an extension of *The Scottish Vowel Length Rule* to pre-stop contexts where, as we saw in Section 3.2(9), it tended not to operate.

Dialectally marked **consonantal** features are relatively rare in Kermack's text, and we only find:

(a) The dental nasal [n] in place of the velar nasal [ŋ] in words like: *damajin* 'damaging'; *lukin* 'looking'; *cheatin* 'cheating'; *shakin* 'shaking' and others. Of course, this is by no means a purely Scots phenomenon, as it is found throughout the English-speaking world in present participle contexts in particular.

(b) [l] vocalisation – an extremely salient feature of modern Central Belt Scots (especially in Working Class male usage) – is only represented once in: *aw day* 'all day'.

(c) The *sumhin* 'something' and *anyhin* 'anything' spellings represent the very salient Working Class Central Belt (but perhaps now spreading wider) phenomenon whereby the interdental voiceless fricative [θ] (the initial sound in 'thick') is realised as [h] (the initial sound in 'house').

But notice how there is no attempt to represent glottal stop usage which, we must suspect, would be a very obvious characteristic in the speech of a character with this social and regional background. Perhaps again the lack of any useable symbol may have been the problem.

The author very successfully represents another characteristic of spontaneous spoken usage, namely the running together of individual words in fast (sometimes called *allegro*) speech, demonstrating how the speech flow is not simply a matter of pronouncing one word in isolation after another. Thus we find: *offy the* 'off of the'; *grainyrice* 'grain of rice'; *hudda loatty* 'had a lot of'; *soze it wizny* 'so as it was not'; *anny* 'and he'; *thottyd* 'thought he'd'.

However, the text is replete with non-standard spellings whose function it is merely to suggest the non-standard and not the Scots non-standard in particular, since they tell us nothing about Scots pronunciation itself. The function of these spellings is presumably one of creating an impression of the spoken as against the written language: *ritten* 'written'; *rite* 'write'; *nite* 'night'; *manijd* 'managed'; *munny* 'money'; *wunce* 'once'; *smollist* 'smallest'; *byro* 'biro'; *swayr* 'swear'; *ize* 'eyes' and many others.

Of course, the author does not merely use pronunciation characteristics to represent the social and regional status of the speaker – syntactic and lexical signals are given as well. Notably, the cliticised negative is in evidence: *kidny* 'couldnae'; *didny* 'didnae', as is the *no* negative: *no much* 'not much'. Again we find the use of the definite article in the way described above in Section 2.1.1: *the invalidity* and the use of the comparative *that*, for the standard *so*, in the phrase *that fully ize* 'so full of eyes'. The vocabulary signals are relatively infrequent and only involve words which are widely and generally recognised as Scots: *tatty* 'potato'; *wee* 'small'; *bairns* 'children'; and *yi ken* 'you know'.

Suggested Reading

*Macafee, I.C. 1982. 'Glasgow dialect in literature'. *Scottish Language* 1, pp. 45–53.

Macaulay, R.K.S. 1991. 'Coz it izny Spelt when they say it. Displaying dialect in writing'. *American Speech* 66, pp. 280–291.

Macaulay, R.K.S. 1988. 'Urbanity in an urban dialect: the poetry of Tom Leonard'. *Studies in Scottish Literature* 23, pp. 150–63.

CHAPTER EIGHT

The History of English in Scotland

8.1. Language in Early Scotland

We know nothing of the language of the earliest people who settled in Scotland many thousands of years ago. The language spoken by the builders of Skara Brae in Shetland or the great megalithic tombs in the Kilmartin valley can only be a matter of complete speculation. It is probably only with the coming of the Romans to Scotland that we have any clues as to the language spoken there (if, indeed, there was only a single language spoken in Scotland at that time). It seems that the people with whom the Romans came into contact in North Britain in the middle of the first century of our era had been speaking a Celtic language for at least one thousand years previously. There are two different types of this Celtic language. One, the ancestor of modern-day Welsh, Cornish (now extinct) and Breton – known as Brythonic (Brython – 'a Briton') – was widely spoken throughout the whole of mainland Britain in the Roman period; in southern Scotland, it took various forms, known as Strathclyde, Rheghed and Gododdin Welsh. In northern Scotland it may have been represented by Pictish, but we cannot be completely certain of this, since there are no surviving written materials in that language. The other – the ancestor of modern Scottish and Irish Gaelic – is usually known as the Geidelic or Goidelic type (Goidel, an Irishman (Gael)). Sometimes these two groups are respectively known as P-Celtic and Q-Celtic from the way they treat the sounds represented by the <p> and <q> symbols. In early Welsh, for instance, the word for 'son' is *map* and the word for 'head' *pen*. In the Q-Celtic group, the [p] sound comes to be altered to what is probably [k] (represented by the symbol <q>); thus, in the Goidelic group, 'son' is *mac* and 'head' is *ceann* (as in Malcolm Canmore 'big head').

As far as can be ascertained with any certainty, at the end of the Roman period the majority of people living in Scotland spoke one of the Brythonic Celtic types (Strathclyde Welsh or Pictish). Although the dating is contentious, from around the beginning of the sixth century (but it may well have been earlier) there was a kind of near-simultaneous linguistic pincer movement involving invasions and settlements from both Ireland and Continental Europe. The former of these involved Gaelic-speaking groups from what is now Ulster, initially settling in Kintyre (with their headquarters at Dunadd in mid-Argyll – Argyll meaning the territory of the Gaels). This group ultimately conquered (or at least assimilated) the Brythonic Picts in the North of Scotland. The other incursion was in the South-East of the country – notably in Berwickshire – and came directly from Continental Europe (probably North Germany or Southern Denmark) possibly after a period of settlement in the North-East of England. This latter group spoke a Germanic language, an ancestor of English, often known as Anglian, which came to be widely used throughout the North of England (and which, of course, gives its name to English). It is this Anglian dialect of English that is the ancestor of Modern Scots.

The archaeological and written sources for the early history of the expansion of English-speaking settlers into Southern Scotland are both sparse and difficult to interpret. The Welsh poet Aneurin describes what appears to have been the conquest by the Angles of the Brythonic Celts and the founding of the Anglian kingdom of Bernicia in the middle of the sixth century. Within one hundred years the Celtic capital of Edinburgh (DunEidyn) had been captured by Angles, and from thence there was a steady (but perhaps piecemeal) expansion of English-speaking settlers northwards and (mainly) north-eastwards. So much so, that by the time of David I there was a major Anglian settlement at Abercorn and by 973 the Lothians had been ceded to these proto-Scots speakers. The push northwards brought conflict with Picts (although an Anglian force under king Egfrith was comprehensively defeated by them at Nechtansmere in 685). The ultimate success of the English-speaking groups was enhanced by two political factors: (a) the policy of David 1 to establish *burghs* across Scotland peopled largely by Scots speakers and (b) the introduction of English-speaking tenants by the Norman nobility. As a result, English (in its Scots form) became the language certainly of administration and government and was used widely in all types of written records, a situation which was complete by the middle of the fourteenth century, when Scots was adopted as the official language of the Scots parliament. Certainly between the eleventh and the fourteenth centuries the form of the English language spoken in Scotland was referred to as *Inglis*, with Gaelic known as *Scots* or *Erse*. In 1376, for example, Androw of Wyntoun in his *Orygynale Cronykil of Scotland* describes the 'langagis of Bretayne' as comprising 'Brettys first, and Inglis syne [since], Pecht, and Scot, and syne Latyne', keeping the distinction between Scots (Gaelic) and Inglis (ancestor of Modern Scots). But by the sixteenth century we begin to see the term 'Scots' used specifically for the descendant of Anglian, and not for Gaelic. Thus in 1596 we have John Leslie writing in his *Historie of Scotland*: 'For the Ingles men, evin as the mair politick Scottis, vses that ald Saxone toung ... quhilke [which] now is called the Ingles toung', and again: 'Quhen [when] Scotis and Inglis language ar neir nychtbouris [neighbours], sounding almaist baith alyk'.

However, we need to stress the multilingual nature of Scotland in the early period. Norwegian invaders had substantial holdings, especially in the North-West of the country, the Hebrides and the Northern Isles, and we must assume that Norse, Gaelic and even Scots existed side by side in a multi-ethnic, multi-linguistic community in many parts of the country. By the fifteenth and centuries, however, there is little doubt that *Inglis* was the official language of the realm and supported a vibrant literary tradition. The language was making considerable inroads, even then, into what remained of the Gaelic- and Norse-speaking parts of the country (notably in Caithness and the Northern Isles). It is important to stress that, even at this early stage in its history, the version of English spoken in Scotland was unaffected by language contact with Gaelic or the Brythonic Pictish. There is very little evidence that there was even much by way of vocabulary borrowing into the embryonic Scots from these languages and no evidence at all for effects on its syntax or morphology.

8.2.1. Periodic Divisions

While they are for guidance only and often have little basis in linguistic fact or development, language histories are often divided into 'periods'. Thus we have Old English (from the earliest sixth century records to 1066); Middle English (1066–1450) (from the Norman Conquest to the end of the Wars of the Roses); early Modern English (1450–1700) (ending around the time of the Glorious Revolution); and late Modern English (1700–1900). Clearly such divisions are somewhat *ad hoc* from a linguistic point of view and reflect political events as much as anything else. There is clearly no sense in which it can be argued that speakers went to bed on December 31st 1065 speaking Old English to awake next morning speaking Middle English! Scots too is traditionally divided into a number of historical periods. These are: (a) **Older Scots** (from the earliest records to 1700). Older Scots is itself divided into three main sub-divisions: *Pre-literary Scots* (Scots to 1375); *Early Scots* (1375–1450); and *Middle Scots* (1450–1700); (b) **Modern Scots** (1700 to the present day). But, as with the English historical divisions, these are not to be taken too literally as reflections of linguistic innovations and change.

Of the very earliest forms of Scots we know almost nothing, largely owing to the extreme paucity of surviving documentary materials. It is perhaps true to say that the very earliest text which survives in Scots (or Proto-Scots) is the Anglian inscription on the magnificent stone cross which still stands today in Ruthwell kirk near Annan in Dumfries and Galloway. The inscription itself is in the Runic alphabet (showing strong Scandinavian influence) and takes the form of a poem, sometimes known as the *Vision of the Cross* or the *Dream of the Rood*. The dating of this inscription is the subject of some controversy, but it is certainly early, possibly around 600AD. A transliteration of the runes (and there is a separate non-runic Anglian version of the poem as well) reveals the Holy Cross speaking:

> Cross was I reared raised I (the) mighty king
> Rod   wæs ic aræred, ahof ic   riicne   cyning

> Heavens' lord   to bend myself not dare (I)
> Heofona hlaford, hyldan   me   ne dorste.

> Driven through they me with   dark   nails
>   þurhdrifan   hi me mid deorcan næglum

This early form of the language is obviously very remote from that used at present and requires separate study to fully comprehend it, but it is possible to recognise words like *cyning* 'king', *Þurh* 'through', *drifan* 'drive', *deorc* 'dark' and *nægl* 'nail', despite the use of specialised alphabet symbols.

Although some Charters show early Scots in the form of place-names, thus *Aschchyrc* 'Ashkirk' (1116), *Strevelinschire* (1130) 'Stirlingshire' (1179), *Kirkpatric, Cludesdale* ('Clydesdale'), *Glencarn* (1179) and *Neuton* 'Newtown' (1189), perhaps the very earliest form of Scots which is readily identifiable as such is that found in a lease document (a *conventio*) made between the Abbot of Scone and the Hays of Leys, dated 1312 (two years before the battle of Bannockburn and fifty years before Chaucer). The Scots language in this text (sometimes called *The Scone Gloss*) appears as an interlinear gloss, i.e. the Scots words are written above their Latin equivalents by way of translation. Thus, for the Latin 'cyrographi', we have the Scots *hand chartir*, 'annuatim'/*iere bi iere* ('year by year'); 'dominio'/*ye laurdscape* ('the lordship'); 'revocare'/*cal again*; 'solebant'/*wer wont.*

Despite the still widespread use of Gaelic and Norman French among the aristocracy and bureaucratic classes, by 1500 Scots had become the official language of court and governmental circles. It had also established itself as the principal medium of communication at all social levels and (increasingly) in all geographical areas of the country as well (even those where Gaelic was still widely spoken). The late

Middle Ages are sometimes considered to be the apogee of Scots, since so much important literature was produced in the language in that period, notably by writers of such stature as Henryson, Dunbar and Douglas among many others. While it is difficult to find a single piece of language absolutely typical of a given period in any language, the following extract from Robert Henryson's famous allegorical poem *The Frog and the Mouse* is a good sample of literary language of the second half of the sixteenth century. The extract describes the final struggle between the two animals and their opportunistic seizure by a hawk:

The dreid of deid hir strenthis gart increß
And fandit hir defend with mony mane.
The mowß upwart, the *paddok* doun can preß;   *frog*
Quhile to, quhile fra, quhile *dowk*, quhile vp agane.

> *sometimes: plunge*

This silly mouß, thus plungit in grit pane,
Can fecht als lang as breth wes in hir breist;
Till at þe last scho cryit for a preist.

Sichand thus gait, a *gled* sat on a *twist*,   *[the mouse] sighing in
                                                  this manner; hawk; branch*
And to þis wrechit battell tuke gud heid;
And with a *wisk, or owþir* of þame *wist*,   *whisk; before
                                                        either; realised*
He *claucht his cluke* betuene þame in the threid;   *closed his
                                                              claw;*
Syne to þe land he flew with þame gud speid,
Fane of þat *fang*, pypand with mony *pew*;   *eager; capture;
                                                         cry of bird*
Syne *lowsit* þame, and bathe *but* pety slew.   *undid; without*
Syne *bowellit* þame, þat bowchir, with his bill, *disembowelled*;
And bellyflawcht full fetly he þame flaid;
Bot baith þair fleache wald skant be half a fill,
And gutis als, vnto þat gredy gled.
Off þair debait thus quhen I hard owt red,
He tuk his flicht, and our þe feildis he flaw:
Gif þis be trew, speir ӡe þat þame at saw.

Spellings: Here again we see some of the specialised symbols like 'þ' (for 'th') which are a feature of the Ruthwell Cross text. However, many printers did not have a symbol like this in their fonts in the Middle Scots period, and the symbol 'y' was often used as a substitute. Thus we can find *ye* for 'the' and *yame* for 'them', although the precise details of the usage are complex. Two other symbols are of interest as well. The symbol 'ß' is no more than a convention for 's' and seems to have no other special significance. However, the 'ȝ' symbol is a different matter. It too is to be found in the very earliest English texts (it is sometimes called 'yogh') and has a pronunciation value equivalent to [j], the first sound in words like 'you' and 'young'. However, it is often the case that, in the Middle Scots period, printers did not have this symbol in their font inventory, and substituted 'z' for it. Thus for a word like *cunȝe* 'coin', we find printers using a spelling like *cunze* or even *cunzie*. This use of the 'z' symbol explains why, in Modern Scots, personal and place names like *Menzies, Dalzell* and *Cockenzie* can have alternative pronunciations, one with the [j] sound, the other with a rationalisation of the 'z' spelling as representing [z]. In this way, for instance, *Dalzell* can be heard pronounced as [dalzɛl] and [daljɛl]. On other occasions, combinations like 'nȝ' were rendered as 'ng' by printers, leading to spelling pronunciations of *Menzies* as [mɪŋɪs] 'mingis' and, even, for *Mackenzie* one like [məkɪnŋje] 'macingye'.

Spellings like *quhile* 'while' in the passage above point to one of the most common characteristics of Middle Scots orthography – namely, the use of 'qu', 'qw' and even 'qhu' for the later 'wh' spelling convention in words like 'who', 'which' and 'what'. In Middle Scots such words are found with spellings like *qhuo/quo* 'who'; *quhome* 'whom'; *quhirill wind* 'whirl wind' and the like. Our passage also shows words spelt with two vowel symbols, thus *dreid, breist, heid* and several others. One might expect that such a double vowel graph would infer the presence of a *diphthong* or double vowel. In fact, most of the evidence we have suggests that the use of the *i* symbol following the vowel was merely a convention to signal that the vowel itself was long rather than short. There is no inference that a diphthong is involved.

Morphology: Among the most obvious characteristics of word structure shown by our text are forms like *fandit* 'found', *plungit* 'plunged', *lousit* 'loosened' and *'cryit* 'cried'. Past tense forms in Modern Scots are produced usually by adding to the right of the verb itself an ending in [t] or [d], thus 'looked' and 'dragged'. Characteristic of the morphology of Middle Scots was the addition of endings spelt 'it' and 'id' (there are, of course, survivals of this usage in Modern Scots as in words like *drookit* 'drenched'), suggesting that the ending was a separate syllable, thus [kraɪət] *cryit* and [plʊnʒət] *plungit.*

The Middle Scots inflectional system for verbs in the present tense seems to have gone like: *I fynd, thou fyndis, she fyndis,* although it is also possible to see *I fyndis* forms as well. There seems to be a convention in the language to the effect that when the verb is separated from its subject, then it will attract the *-is* ending, thus: *I rede wele oft and kepis* 'I read very often and keep' where the first verb shows no ending, the second attracting the *is* inflection.

The full-syllable status of some endings in Middle Scots is to be found as well in the way it forms the plurals of nouns. While the modern language uses suffixes like [s] and [z] as in 'cats' and 'dogs', Middle Scots can show spellings like *moderis* 'mothers', *bukis* 'books' and, in our passage, *strenthis* 'strengths' and *feildis* 'fields'. There is much controversy as to whether these *is* endings were pronounced as separate syllables, but there is strong evidence to suggest that, in verse forms at least, they indeed had a separate syllabic value in [əs]. Finally, forms like *sichand* and *pypand* in our passage show the Middle Scots use of the *–and* suffix for the present participle, where Middle English and Modern English varieties as a whole use an *-ing* form.

Pronunciation: The details of Middle Scots pronunciation are too complex to deal with in a short work like this, but a few observations are worth making, especially as regards consonants. Very often we find that there has been a change from [ð] (as in 'the') to [d]: thus we have forms like *moderis* 'mothers' and *faderis* 'fathers' appearing quite frequently. Likewise, the use of the [l] sound in Middle Scots is quite distinctive. We have already seen how, in Modern Scots, [l] at the end of words and syllables can be *vocalised* [§5.3: p. 56], so that we get [tuo] for 'tool' and so on. This phenomenon is current in Middle Scots as well. However, we also find in Scots of that period the opposite process taking place, that is where [l] sounds seem to be added in contexts where they do not historically belong (the **intrusive 'l'**). In this way we can find spellings like *walkit* 'waked', *altar* 'author' and *waltir* 'water'. However, some scholars argue that this 'l' symbol was not pronounced, but inserted merely as an orthographic convention to signal that the vowel preceding it was long. Consider Middle Scots spellings such as *chamer/chaamer/chalmer* 'a room' or 'chamber'. The *al* and the *aa* spellings we might regard as equivalent, signifying vowel length. The modern pronunciation of the 'l' sound in *Chalmers* probably merely represents a later, spelling-based pronunciation.

8.2.2. Anglicisation

It is often argued that by the sixteenth century the distinctive form of English spoken in Scotland was beginning to be diluted under the influence of the English spoken in England itself. It is often sometimes claimed too that the tendency to produce an anglicised form of the language was enhanced by John Knox's use of the Geneva version of the Bible, a work written in the Standard English of the time. For the want of a version of Scripture of a more Scots-specific variety, the daily use of this English-language version, it is argued, led to a diminution in the status of Scots itself. Some writers suggest that this marked the beginnings of the **anglicisation** of Scots, a process which many see as ongoing since that time. However, we need not accept this point of view unequivocally. In the first place, it is difficult to see how an entire population could change its day-to-day speech habits under the influence of the language of a document they may only have heard read on specific occasions and in specific contexts. We do not know either the type of accent the English Bible may have been read aloud in from the pulpit. Nor can we assume that the clergy were, at that time, familiar – to any significant degree – with the usage of English speakers south of the border. Even today, when large sections of the population who speak distinctive regional forms of English are, on an everyday basis, exposed to spoken Standard English on television and radio, there is little evidence suggesting that their speech habits are being substantively affected by it.

It is certainly true that there was much controversy about the use and appropriateness of Scots terminology and phraseology in religious discourse from the earliest beginnings of the Reformation in Scotland. From the sixteenth through to the eighteenth century a considerable controversy raged between Episcopalian and Presbyterian supporters (largely carried out through widely distributed pamphlets) concerning the appropriateness of the use of Scots in religious contexts. In 1692 one Gilbert Crockatt produced an ironic tract entitled *The Scotch Presbyterian Eloquence Displayd*. This set out to ridicule and criticise the language used by Presbyterians in their dealings with their congregations. What were felt to be Scotticisms were bowdlerised, with overtly Scots words like *bonny, midden, lang syne, moss, whaup* seen by the Episcopalians as examples of the foolishness of the teaching used by the Presbyterians. Yet what was known as this 'homely style' of the Presbyterians had its supporters, notably in George Ridpath. In his pamphlet of 1693 entitled *Ane Answer to the Scotch Presbyterian Eloquence*, Ridpath asserts how 'no Scots Man can approve our Authors ridiculing his own Country Language [and I hope] that Pious Church of *England* Men will have no less esteeme for our Scotch Preachers that they speak intelligibly to the People, no more than they would for a good Sermon, if dressed in *Yorkshire* or *Cornish* Phrase'.

However, there was indeed one context where anglicisation was quite prevalent in this period, and that was in the conventions used in the **written** form of the language. Throughout the Middle Ages, there was no accepted national written standard of English, either in England or in Scotland. It is only in the later fifteenth century that we find a standard written form of English being used in official court and government documents in England itself. Before then, there appears to have been a set of different **regional written standards**. Perhaps as a direct result of the move of the Scottish Court to London in 1603, the written form of Scottish English takes on an appearance similar to that of written English texts. Characteristically Scottish spelling forms – notably 'qu-' for 'wh-' in words like *quhilk* 'which', *quhen* 'when', *ane* for 'an', *nocht* for 'not', *goand* for 'going' and *endit* for 'ended' – become less and less prominent in texts written in Scotland so that by the beginning of the seventeenth century they all but disappear. Yet this in no way infers that such forms were still not widespread in *spoken* usage.

It is perhaps too readily assumed that the Scots used by modern educated Middle Class speakers somehow represents an anglicisation based upon contact with Standard English itself. Even a cursory glance at some of the most salient characteristics of the former – its use of the [a] vowel in 'bath' words and the monophthong in 'say' and 'go' in contrast to the very salient Standard English diphthongs in such words – suggests that this assumption is not based on solid foundations. The allegation that a Standard English-influenced Middle Class Scots has come into being is usually based on evidence from the eighteenth and nineteenth centuries. In that era of linguistic prescriptivism, Scots was seen as an inferior language, in need of purification and regularisation on the model of the southern English court standard form. But the evidence from the eighteenth and nineteenth centuries (and it is extensive) in fact suggests that – while there was indeed a tendency to wish to see Scots 'improved' – what was held up as the model on which this improvement was to be based was not some southern English form, but rather (and quite explicitly) an overtly *Scots* Middle Class form – the 'language of the College, the Pulpit and the Bar'. This 'Caledonian English' had a very high prestige in Scotland itself, far outweighing anything that might be seen as an English import. And it is from that eighteenth-century Caledonian English (essentially an upper social class prestige dialect) that much modern Middle Class

Scots itself directly descends. But even at the height of this eighteenth-century linguistic cleansing in Scotland there was a strong tendency (very much in the tradition of that of Ridpath a century earlier) supporting the retention of spoken and written *broad* Scots, probably essentially a non-urban usage, a movement which saw proselytisers in Burns, Fergusson, Geddes and, a century later, Walter Scott.

8.3. Some Important Historical Linguistic Developments

There are some major developments which took place in the history of Scots which can serve to explain some of the differences between the modern language and other varieties of English and, at the same time, explain divergences (especially inter-dialectal ones) within modern Scots itself. The developments we shall examine here have to do with pronunciation, but there were important historical developments as well in the language's morphology, syntax and vocabulary. There are two major pronunciation innovations in the history of Scots which are of especial significance. One of these we have already discussed: *The Scottish Vowel Length Rule* (§3.2(9) above). However, if there is one single historical process which has a major effect on the subsequent development of the English language in general (and its effect on Scots is considerable as well), then it is *The Great Vowel Shift*. This process had a major impact on the development of the pronunciation of (particularly long) vowels and is, indeed, still operative in much of Modern English pronunciation. The fact that Modern Scots still has pronunciations like 'coo', 'noo' and 'hoose' and, in some regions, shows 'sick' and 'seek', 'mate' and 'meat' as homophones, largely stems from the way *The Great Vowel Shift* has operated (or failed to operate) in the English of Scotland.

The Great Vowel Shift is a complex process and we can only offer a general summary of it here. Consider words such as *bite, beet, beat* and *abate*. Modern English spelling is not always a good guide to current pronunciation but in many ways quite accurately reflects Standard English pronunciation in earlier periods (perhaps most notably that of the sixteenth and seventeenth centuries when our modern spelling system began to be standardised in the shape it is now). The spelling of these words suggests that they were all pronounced differently at some point in their history. The following table gives a (simplified) account of what the pronunciations of long front vowels might have been like between 1400 and, say, 1600:

Modern spellings	1400 pronunciations	1400 Vowel Heights	1500 Vowel Heights	1500 pronuncations
bite	[ii] the vowel in 'see': [biit]	High	Rising Diphthong	[bəɪt]
beet	[ee] the vowel in 'say': [beet]	High Mid	High	[biit]
beat	[ɛɛ] the vowel in 'get': [bɛɛt]	Low Mid	High Mid	[beet]
abate	[aa] the vowel in 'cat': [əbaat]	Low	Low Mid	[əbɛɛt]

Two separate things seem to be happening to the long vowel sounds. In the first place, the *high vowel [ii] is changed into a diphthong* [əɪ] (a sound close to the modern Standard English diphthong in words like 'my', 'tie' and 'find'). Secondly, it would appear that *the other vowels have all raised by one height*, so that high-mid has become high ([beet] → [biit]), low-mid become high-mid ([bɛɛt] → [beet]) and low become low-mid ([baat] → [bɛɛt]). It is this combined raising and diphthongisation process that is known as either *The Great Vowel Shift* or *The English Vowel Shift*. Notice too how, since 1500, the vowels in *beet* and *beat* have fallen together (merged) under [ii]. On the other hand, the stressed vowel in *abate* has merged with that of the newly raised *beat*, under [ee].

This *raising and diphthongisation process* affected the long back vowels as well, so that words which pre-1500 showed the long low back [ɑɑ] vowel in words like *ham* as in 'Birmingham'

have subsequently been raised to the [oo] (through an intermediate low mid [ɔɔ] stage) to appear as *home*. In some varieties
of Scots, this [oo] has undergone further raising to [uu] as in
the Scots pronunciation of *home* as in the personal name *Hume*.
Indeed, the eighteenth-century philosopher, David Hume,
changed his family name from its usual form *Home* to *Hume*
because of 'thae glaekit English bodies, who could not call him
aright'. Obviously the change from [oo] to [uu] had not
occurred in southern English at this time (or subsequently).

There are some other specifically Scots idiosyncrasies relating to *The Great Vowel Shift* which are worth noting. In the
first place, we have shown above how words whose spelling
suggests they have some kind of low vowel, see this vowel
raised to [oo] or [uu]. Thus, a word like *stone* – spelt *stan* in
early English – is a good example of a word which originally
had a low back [ɑɑ] vowel raised (probably very early in the
history of English and Scots) to [oo], hence the *stone* spelling.
However, in many Scots dialects there appears to have been
another, earlier change whereby the low back [ɑɑ] vowel was
fronted to [aa] (a change from the vowel in Standard English
bath to the vowel in *cat*). The [aa] vowel in its turn was
subjected to *The Great Vowel Shift*, showing raising of the
vowel to [ee], thus the Modern Scots (social and regional)
alternation between [ston] and [sten] 'stane'. This process
gives rise too to the [e] pronunciation in Scots of words like
sore and *more* – [ser] and [mer].

But perhaps the most obviously Scots aspect of *The Great
Vowel Shift* lies in the way it treats the long high back [uu]
vowel. We already noted how high front vowels like [ii]
become diphthongs, thus the spelling *mine* but the diphthongal pronunciation in Standard English of [aɪ] or, in some
Scots dialects – [ʌɪ]. In the same way, the high long back vowel
[uu] diphthongises in Standard English to [ɑu], so that we find
a diphthong in words like *house*, *mouth* and *mouse*, words
which, in the earliest English, were spelt *hus*, *muþ* and *mus*. But
in many regional and social dialects of Scots (as well as North-
Eastern English) this diphthongisation of [uu] has not occurred, speakers still producing pronunciations like [hus], [muθ]

and [mus] (although the vowels in Scots tend to be fronted to [ü]).

There are other aspects of modern Scots pronunciation which illustrate peculiarly Scots manifestations of *The Great Vowel Shift*. Notably in some urban dialects, the vowel in words like *beat* and *treat* has not undergone the expected raising to [ii], but remained at [ee].

The history of the English language in Scotland is, of course, not complete, it never stops. Changes to all aspects of the grammar are ongoing at all times and in all parts of the country. Some of these we have touched upon in Chapter Five. However, we are not yet in a position to predict which changes will gain the most ground and which features of the current grammatical structure will disappear or become residual. On the basis of current research it does seem, however, that many changes are being led by adolescents, possibly most readily by females and those at the Working Class/Middle Class boundary. It seems, too, that a certain degree of levelling is taking place between these speakers, so that many of the language features (perhaps especially in pronunciation) which had earlier characterised them are being neutralised and a new 'bland' dialect is being formed. A phenomenon like this appears to be occurring in many parts of England, and there is every reason to believe that it is happening in Scotland as well, although much more research effort, time and financial support needs to be provided in this important area.

Suggested Reading

Jones, C. 1996. *A Language Suppressed*. Edinburgh. John Donald.

Jones, C. 1997. ed. *The Edinburgh History of the Scots Language*. Edinburgh. Edinburgh University Press.

*Robinson, M. 1985. 'A History of Scots', in *The Concise Scots Dictionary*. Aberdeen. Aberdeen University Press, pp. ix–xvi.

*Templeton, J.M. 1973. 'Scots: an outline history', in A.J. Aitken. ed. *Lowland Scots*, pp. 4–19.

Supplementary Reading

General Scots

Aitken, A.J. 1973. ed. *Lowland Scots*. Association for Scottish Literary Studies. Occasional Papers. Edinburgh.

Aitken, A.J. 1984. 'Scots and English in Scotland', in Trudgill, P. ed. *Language in the British Isles*. Cambridge. Cambridge University Press, pp. 517–32.

Aitken, A.J. and McArthur, T. 1979. eds. *Languages of Scotland*. Edinburgh. Edinburgh University Press.

Aitken, A.J., McIntosh, A. and Pálsson, H. 1971. eds. *Edinburgh Studies in English and Scots*. London. Longman.

Bald, M. 1927. 'The Pioneers of Anglicised Speech in Scotland'. *Scottish Historical Review* 25, pp. 163–179.

Durkacz, V.E. 1983. *The Decline of the Celtic Languages*. Edinburgh. John Donald.

Görlach, M. 1985. ed. *Focus on Scotland*. Amsterdam.

Grant, W. and Main-Dixon, J. 1921. *Manual of Modern Scots*. Cambridge. Cambridge University Press.

Hardie, K. 1995/96. 'Scots: matters of identity and nationalism'. *Scottish Language* 14/15, 141–147.

Macafee, C.I. 1983. *Varieties of English Around the World: Glasgow*. Amsterdam. Benjamin.

Mather, J.Y. 1973. 'The Scots we speak today', in Aitken, A.J. ed. *Lowland Scots: Occasional papers No. 2*. Edinburgh. Association for Scottish Literary Studies, pp. 56–71.

McClure, J.D. 1979. 'Scots, its range of uses', in Aitken, A.J. and McArthur, T. eds. *Languages of Scotland*. Edinburgh. Edinburgh University Press, pp. 26–48.

McClure, J.D. 1983. ed. *Scotland and the Lowland Tongue*. Aberdeen. Aberdeen University Press.

McClure, J.D. 1985. 'Scottis, Inglis, Suddron: language labels and language attitudes', in Görlach, M. ed. *Focus on Scotland*. Amsterdam. Benjamin, pp. 52–69.

McClure, J.D. 1994. 'English in Scotland', in Burchfield, R. ed. *Cambridge History of the English Language*. Vol. V. Cambridge. Cambridge University Press.

McClure, J.D. and Spiller, M.R.G. 1989. eds. *Bryght Lanternis: Essays on the Language and Literature of Mediaeval and Renaissance Scotland*. Aberdeen. Aberdeen University Press.

Mather, J.Y. 1973. 'The Scots we speak today', in Aitken, A.J. ed. *Lowland Scots: Occasional papers No. 2*. Edinburgh. Association for Scottish Literary Studies, pp. 56–71.

Meier, Hans H. 1977. 'Scots is not alone: the Swiss and Low German Analogues', in Aitken, A.J. *et al.* eds. *Bards and Makars*. Glasgow. University Press, pp. 201–13.

Melchers, G. 1985. '"Knappin', "Proper English", "Modified Scottish": Some language attitudes in the Shetland Isles', in Görlach, M. ed. 1985, pp. 87–100.

Melchers, G. 1991. 'Norn-Scots: a complicated language contact situation in Shetland', in Ureland, Sture, P. and Broderick, George. eds. *Language Contact in the British Isles*. Tübingen. Niemayer, pp. 461–77.

Menzies, J. 1991. 'An investigation of attitudes to Scots and Glasgow dialect among secondary school pupils'. *Scottish Language* 10, pp. 30–46.

Miller, J. 1985. Review of C. Macafee. *Varieties of English Around the World: Glasgow. Scottish Language* 4, pp. 32–36.

Murdoch, S. 1995. *Language Politics in Scotland*. Aberdeen University Scots Leid Quorum.

Sandred, K.I. 1983. *Good or bad Scots?* Stockholm. Almqvist & Wiksell.

Trotter, R. de B. 1901. 'The Scottish Language'. *The Gallovidian* vol. 3, pp. 22–29.

Sounds and Syntax

Aitken, A.J. 1981. 'The Scottish Vowel-Length Rule', in Benskin, M. and Samuels, M.L. eds. *So Meny People Longages and Tonges: Philological Essays in Scots and Mediaeval English Presented to Angus McIntosh*. Edinburgh. Edinburgh University Press, pp. 131–57.

Brown, E.K. and Miller, J. 1982. 'Aspects of Scottish English syntax'. *English World-Wide* 3, pp. 3–17.

Brown, G. 1979. *Intonation of Scottish English*. SSRC Final Report. London.

Currie, K. 1979. *Intonation Systems of Scottish English*. Ph.D. Dissertation. Edinburgh.

Gburek, H. 1984. 'Changes in the structure of the English verb system: Evidence from Scots'. *Scottish Studies* 4, pp. 115–123.

Kohler, K.J. 1966. *Aspects of the History of English Pronunciation in Scotland*. Ph.D. Dissertation. Edinburgh.

Macafee, C.I. 1997. 'Ongoing change in Modern Scots: The social dimension', in Jones, C. ed. *The Edinburgh History of the Scots Language*. Edinburgh. Edinburgh University Press, pp. 514–548.

MacMahon, A.M.S. 1991. 'Lexical Phonology and sound change: the Case of the *Scottish Vowel Length Rule*'. *Journal of Linguistics* 27, pp. 29–53.

Miller, J. 1993. 'The grammar of Scottish English', in Milroy, J. and Milroy, L. eds. *Real English: The grammar of English dialects in the British Isles*. Harlow. Longman, pp. 99–138.

Sabban, A. 1985. 'On the variability of Hebridean English syntax: the verbal group', in Görlach, M. ed. *Focus on Scotland*. Amsterdam. Benjamin, pp. 125–43.

Vianna-Taylor, M. 1974. 'The great southern Scots conspiracy: patterns in the development of Northern English', in Anderson, J.M. and Jones, C. 1974. eds. *Historical Linguistics*. 2 vols. Amsterdam. North Holland, pp. 403–406.

Vocabulary

Agutter, A.J.L and Cowan, L.N. 1981. 'Changes in the vocabulary of Lowland Scots Dialects'. *Scottish Literary Journal*. Supplement 14, pp. 49–62.

Aitken, A.J. *et al*. eds. *A Dictionary of the Older Scottish Tongue*. London. University of Chicago Press.

Robinson, M. 1985. ed. *The Concise Scots Dictionary*. Aberdeen. Aberdeen University Press.

Tulloch, G. 1997. 'Lexis', in Jones, C. ed. *The Edinburgh History of the Scots Language*. Edinburgh. Edinburgh University Press, pp. 378–432.

Language and Society

Aitken, A.J. 1982. 'Bad Scots: some superstitions about Scots speech', *Scottish Language* 1, pp. 30–44.

Cheshire, J. 1991. ed. *English Around the World: Sociolinguistic Perspectives*. Cambridge. Cambridge University Press.

Johnston, P.A. 1983a. *A Sociolinguistic Investigation of Edinburgh Speech*. Social Science Research Council End of Grant Report. C/ 00/23/0023/1.

Johnston, P.A. 1983b. 'Irregular style variation patterns in Edinburgh speech'. *Scottish Language* 2, pp. 1–19.

Johnston, P.A. 1984. 'Variation in the Standard Scottish English of Morningside'. *English World Wide* 2, pp. 133–85.

Johnston, P.A. 1985. 'The rise and fall of the Morningside/Kelvinside accent', in Görlach, M. *Focus on Scotland*. Amsterdam. Benjamin, pp. 37–56.

Macafee, C.I. 1987. 'Language and modern life: notes from Glasgow', in Macafee, C. and Macleod, I. eds. *The Nuttis Schell. Essays on the Scots Language presented to A.J. Aitken*. Aberdeen. Aberdeen University Press, pp. 182–94.

Macafee, C.I. 1988. *Some Studies in the Glasgow Vernacular*. Ph.D. Dissertation. University of Glasgow.

Macafee, C.I. 1991. 'How it feels to be thick as a brick', in Fenton, A. and MacDonald, D.A. eds. *Studies in Scots and Gaelic: Proceedings of the Third Annual Conference on the Languages of Scotland*. Edinburgh. Canongate Academic, pp. 111–17.

Macafee, C.I. 1994a. 'Dialect erosion with special reference to urban Scots', in Fenton, A. and Macdonald, D.A. eds. *Studies in Scots and Gaelic*. Edinburgh. Canongate Academic, pp. 69–80.

Macafee, C.I. 1994b. *Traditional Dialect in the Modern World: A Glasgow Case Study. Bamberger Beiträge zur Englischen Sprachwissenschaft* 35. Frankfurt am Main. Lang.

Macaulay, R. 1985. 'The narrative skills of a Scottish coal miner', in Görlach, M. ed. *Focus on Scotland*. Amsterdam. Benjamin, pp. 101–124.

Macaulay, R. 1991. *Locating Dialect in Discourse: the Language of Honest Men and Bonny Lasses in Ayr*. Oxford. Oxford University Press.

Macaulay, R.K.S. 1977. *Language, Social Class and Education: A Glasgow Study*. Edinburgh. Edinburgh University Press.

Macaulay, R.K.S. 1978. 'Variation and consistency in Glaswegian English', in Trudgill, P. *Sociolinguistic Patterns in British English*. London. Edward Arnold, pp. 132–43.

Macaulay, R.K.S. 1996. 'Remarkably common eloquence: the aesthetics of urban dialect'. *Scottish Language* 14/15, pp. 66–80.

Macaulay, R.K.S. and Trevelyan, G.D. 1977. *Language, Social Class and Education. A Glasgow Study*. Edinburgh. Edinburgh University Press.

Pollner, C. 1985a. *Englisch in Livingston. Ausgewälte sprachliche Erscheinungen in einer schottischen new town*. Frankfurt. Peter Lang.

Pollner, C. 1985b. 'Linguistic fieldwork in a Scottish new town', in Görlach, M. ed. *Focus on Scotland*. Amsterdam. Benjamin, pp. 57–68.

Pollner, C. 1985c. 'Old words in a young town'. *Scottish Language* 4, pp. 5–15.

Reid, E. 1976. *Social and Stylistic Variation in the Speech of Some Edinburgh Schoolchildren*. M.Litt. Dissertation. University of Edinburgh.

Reid, E. 1978. 'Social and stylistic variation in the speech of children', in Trudgill, P. ed. *Sociolinguistic Patterns in British English*. London. Edward Arnold, pp. 158–172.

Romaine, S. 1975. *Linguistic Variability in the Speech of Some Edinburgh Schoolchildren*. M.Litt. Dissertation. University of Edinburgh.

Romaine, S. 1978. 'Postvocalic /r/ in Scottish English: sound change in progress?', in Trudgill, P. ed. *Sociolinguistic Patterns in British English*. London. Edward Arnold, pp. 144–157.

Romaine, S, 1979a. 'The language of Edinburgh schoolchildren: the acquisition of sociolinguistic competence'. *Scottish Literary Journal*, Supplement 9, pp. 54–60.

Romaine, S. 1979b. 'The historical background', in Aitken, A.J. and McArthur, T. 1979. eds. *Languages of Scotland*. Association for Scottish Literary Studies. Occasional Papers 4. Edinburgh. Chambers, pp. 2–13.

Romaine, S. 1980. 'The relative clause marker in Scots English: Diffusion, complexity, and style as dimensions of syntactic change'. *Language in Society* 9, pp. 221–47.

Romaine, S. 1982a. *Socio-Historical Linguistics: its Status and Methodology*. Cambridge. Cambridge University Press.

Romaine, S. 1982b. 'The English language in Scotland', in Bailey, R.W. and Görlach, M. eds. *English as a World Language*, pp. 56–83. Ann Arbor. University of Michigan Press.

Romaine, S. 1984. 'The sociolinguistic history of [t/d] deletion'. *Folia Linguistica Historica* 5, pp. 221–255.

Trudgill, P. 1978. ed. *Sociolinguistic Patterns in British English*. London. Edward Arnold.

Regional Variation

Abercrombie, David. 1979. 'The accents of Standard English in Scotland', in Aitken, A. J. and McArthur, T. eds. *Languages of Scotland*, pp. 68–813. Edinburgh. Edinburgh University Press.

Adams, G.B. 1986. 'Language and man in Ireland', in Barry, M. and Tilling, P.M. eds. *The English Dialects of Ulster*. Holywood, Down. The Ulster Folk and Transport Museum, pp. 17–24.

Barry, M. and Tilling, P.M. 1986. eds. *The English Dialects of Ulster*. Holywood, Down. The Ulster Folk and Transport Museum.

111

Catford, J.C. 1957a. 'The Linguistic Survey of Scotland'. *Orbis*, 6, pp. 105–21.

Catford, J.C. 1957b. 'Vowel systems of Scots dialects'. *Transactions of the Philological Society*, pp. 107–17.

Chambers, J.K. and Trudgill, P. 1980. *Dialectology*. Cambridge. Cambridge University Press.

Dorian, N.C. 1978. *East Sutherland Gaelic*. Dublin Institute for Advanced Studies.

Dorian, N.C. 1981. *Language Death: the Life Cycle of a Scottish Gaelic Dialect*. Philadelphia. University of Pennsylvania Press.

Glauser, B. 1974. *The Scottish-English Linguistic Border*. Bern. Francke.

Görlach, M. 1991. 'Jamaica and Scotland – bilingual or bidialectal', in M. Görlach. ed. *Englishes: Studies in Varieties of English 1984–1988*. Amsterdam. Benjamin, pp. 69–89.

Gregg, R. 1985. *The Scotch-Irish Dialect Boundaries in the Province of Ulster*. Ottawa. Canadian Federation for the Humanities.

Harris, J. 1984. 'English in the North of Ireland', in Trudgill, P. ed. *Language in the British Isles*. Cambridge. Cambridge University Press.

Harris, J. 1985. *Phonological Variation and Change: Studies in Hiberno-English*. Cambridge. Cambridge University Press.

Harris, J. 1993. 'The grammar of Irish English', in Milroy, J. and Milroy, L. eds. *Real English: The Grammar of English Dialects in the British Isles*. Harlow. Longman, pp 139–186.

Hettinga, J. 1981. 'Standard and dialect in Anstruther and Cellardyke'. *Scottish Literary Journal*, Supplement 14, pp. 37–48.

Hughes, G.A. and Trudgill, P. 1987. *English Accents and Dialects*. London. Edward Arnold.

Milroy, J. 1982. 'Some connections between Galloway and Ulster speech'. *Scottish Language* 1, pp. 23–9.

Milroy, J. and Milroy, L. 1993. eds. *Real English: The Grammar of English Dialects in the British Isles*. Harlow. Longman.

Munro, M. 1985. *The Patter: A Guide to Current Glasgow Usage*. Glasgow. Glasgow District Libraries.

Munro, M. 1988. *The Patter: Another Blast*. Edinburgh. Canongate.

Shuken, C.R. 1985. 'Variation in Hebridean English', in Görlach, M. ed. *Focus on Scotland*. Amsterdam. Benjamin, pp. 145–58.

Speitel, H.H. 1969a. *Some Studies in the Dialect of Midlothian*. Ph.D. Dissertation. University of Edinburgh.

Speitel, H.H. 1969b. 'An early specimen of Edinburgh speech'. *Work in Progress*. Department of Phonetics and Linguistics. University of Edinburgh 3, pp. 26–36.

Stuart, Jamie. 1992. *The Glasgow Gospel*. Edinburgh. Saint Andrew Press.

Tilling, P.M. 1986. 'The English dialects of Ulster', in Barry, M. and Tilling, P.M. 1986. eds. *The English Dialects of Ulster*. Holywood, Down. The Ulster Folk and Transport Museum, pp. 1–32.

Wells, J.C. 1982. *Accents of English*. 3 vols. Cambridge. Cambridge University Press.

Wickens, B. 1980. 'Caithness speech'. *Scottish Literary Journal*, Supplement 12, pp. 61–76; Supplement 14. 1981, pp. 25–36.

Wilson, J. 1926. *The Dialects of Central Scotland*. Oxford. Oxford University Press.

Scots in Literary Texts

Donaldson, W. 1986. *Popular Literature in Victorian Scotland*. Aberdeen. Aberdeen University Press.

Donaldson, W. 1989. *The Language of the People. Scots Prose from the Victorian Revival*. Aberdeen. Aberdeen University Press.

Görlach, M. 1987. 'Lexical loss and lexical survival: the case of Scots and English'. *Scottish Language* 6, pp. 1–20.

Hewitt, L. 1992. *A Sociolinguistic Approach to the Study of Literary Dialect in the Work of John Galt and Christian Johnstone*. Ph.D. Dissertation. University of Glasgow.

Macafee, C. 1982. 'Glasgow dialect in literature'. *Scottish Language*. I, pp. 45–53.

History of Scots

Aitken, A.J. 1979. 'Scottish speech: a historical view with special reference to the standard English of Scotland', in Aitken, A.J. and McArthur, T. eds. *Languages of Scotland*. Edinburgh. Chambers, pp. 85–118.

Jones, C. 1996. *A Language Suppressed*. Edinburgh. John Donald.

Jones, C. 1997. ed. *The Edinburgh History of the Scots Language*. Edinburgh. Edinburgh University Press.

McClure, J.D. 1994. 'English in Scotland', in Burchfield, R. ed. *The Cambridge History of the English Language*. London. Cambridge University Press, pp. 23–93.

Sounds and the Symbols Used to Represent Them

Here, for convenience, are set out some of the common sounds of Standard English with symbols used to represent them taken from *The International Phonetic Alphabet*.

Consonantal Sounds

Stop sounds
[b] as in *b*it
[p] as in *p*it
[d] as in *d*own
[t] as in *t*own
[g] as in *g*own
[k] as in *c*lown
[ʔ] as in some Scottish English wa*t*er

Fricative sounds
[v] as in *v*ine
[f] as in *f*ine
[z] as in *z*oo
[s] as in *S*ue
[ð] as in *th*y
[θ] as in *th*igh
[dʒ] as in *ju*dg*e
[tʃ] as in *ch*ur*ch*
[ʒ] as in azure
[ʃ] as in *sh*oe
[ç] as in Scots ni*ch*t
[x] as in Scots lo*ch*

Sonorant sounds
[l] as in *l*ick
[ɫ] as in *l*uck
[m] as in *m*ine
[n] as in mi*n*e
[ŋ] as in si*ng*

[r] as in *r*un

Vowel-like Sounds
[w] as in *w*e
[ʍ] as in Scots *wh*ale
[j] as in *y*ou
[h] as in *h*ouse

Vowel Sounds

(A) Simple Vowels
(1) Vowels formed in the Front of the Mouth (Unrounded)
High tongue position

[i] as in s*ee*

Mid Tongue position

[e] as in Scots s*ay*:

NB: In such words this sound is not found in Standard English; the diphthong [eɪ] is used instead.

[ɛ] as in g*e*t

Low Tongue position

[a] as in c*a*t

(2) Vowels formed in the Back of the Mouth (Rounded)
High tongue position

[u] as in y*ou*

Mid Tongue position

[o] as in Scots g*o*

NB: In such words this sound is not found in Standard English; the diphthong [ou] is used instead.

[ɔ] as in g*o*t

Low Tongue position

[ɑ] as in Standard English b*a*th, f*a*ther and p*a*th.

(B) Complex Vowel Sounds
Diphthongs
(a) Where first element is lower than the second
(rising diphthongs)
[eɪ] as in Standard English s*ay*

[aɪ] as in m*y*

[ou] as in Standard English g*o*

[ɔɪ] as in b*oy*

[au] as in h*ou*se

(b) Where first element is lower than the second
(**falling diphthong**)

[iə] as in h*e*re and n*ea*r.

[ɛə] as in th*e*re, w*e*re.
(in both cases, the final [r] has been lost in Standard English (but not in Scots varieties))

Index